AF484668

Written from the depths of trauma and pain
Pen to paper, thought to word
The darkness dimmed
And the light began to emerge

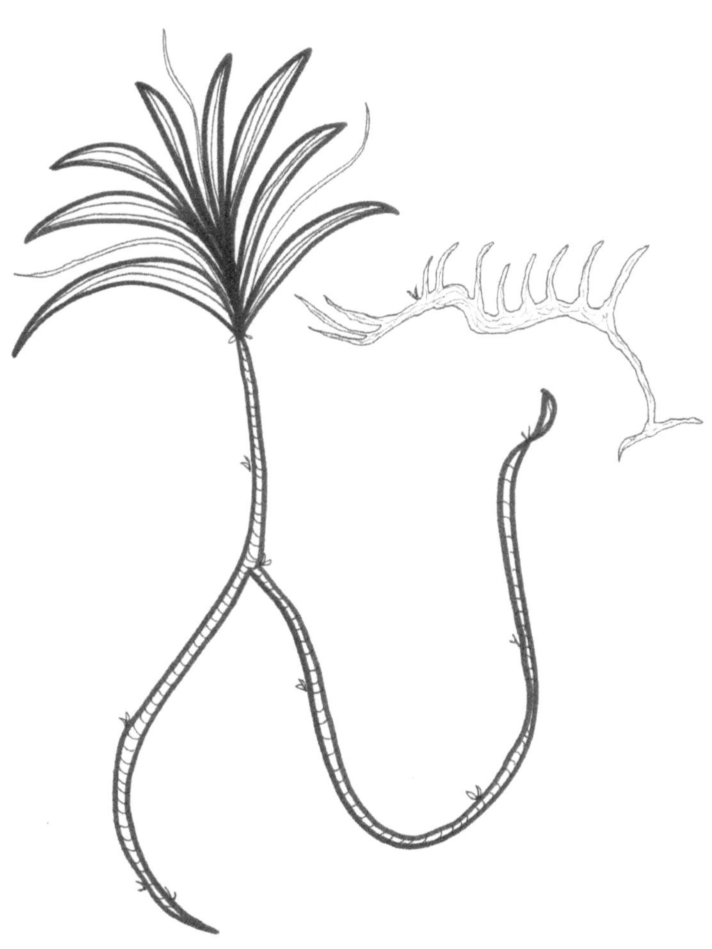

DEDICATION

To my family, friends and loved ones.
To the justice makers, the peacekeepers,
the singers, artists, the castaways and way seekers. To the
pillars of strength forging forward before us.
To those who dare to create and pursue their dreams
and aspirations despite fear and darkness.
To caregivers, tree planters, nature protectors,
lifesavers and lost souls. To wanderers and wonderers.
To the warriors of truth and the holders of the light.

INTRODUCTION

"Write about what you know." That was my daily instruction to hundreds of high school students I worked with in a 34 year career teaching English in a New Jersey public high school.

Little did I expect that some 32 years later I would receive a phone call from a former student who had apparently been doing just that and who was self-publishing a book of her poetry and drawings based on her experiences, both traumatic and inspirational.

Rachel Conanan Delgado was a student of mine in Honors English 1,2,3 and in Humanities and Journalism some thirty years ago. In July of 2022, she called to tell me that she never forgot my advice about writing and to thank me for encouraging her to write, as I often told her I thought she was one of the best writers in class.

At first, I was stunned to both hear from a student whom I had so long ago and to hear a little about her life as it had unfolded after high school. She shared some details about a traumatic experience she had had as a child, which became part of her evolution as a writer of poems and as a writer of music and as a performing musician. I remembered vividly that she had lost her mother the year she entered the high school as an 8th grader and I had her in my class for the first time. Her process of writing was unfolding then, probably before she even knew it and apparently continued in both the creation of poems, music lyrics, and drawings up to this day.

When she asked me to read her work, I was honored. In her poetry and drawings, Rachel has managed to find light in the darkness of her experiences, to find transformation in knowledge about her past, and to find hope for her future as a creative chronicler of her life.

This collection is both a tribute to the power of words and the power of truth, to the writing and expression of what we know and how we remember it. As Maya Angelou said, "There is no greater agony than bearing an untold story inside you."

With her work in this book, Rachel tells her story and unleashes her agony. We look forward to hearing about where this will take her.

Rose De Poto   4/17/2023

Your experience
Is a gift
That when shared
Keeps giving

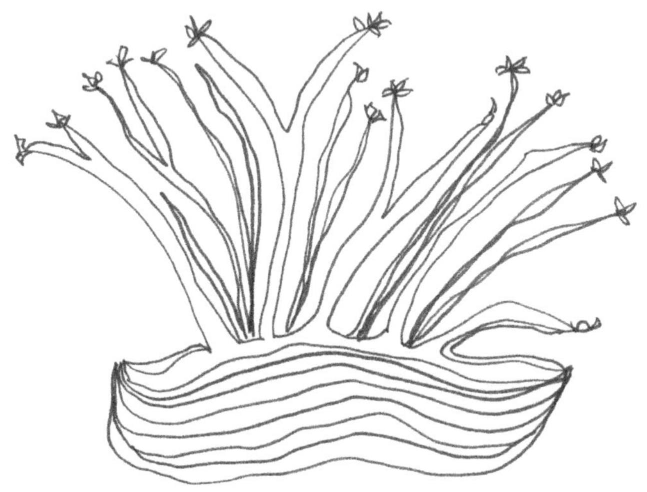

CONTENTS

Poem
Flower
Showing
Power

Nonsense
Sour
Lengthened
Hours

Words
Birds
Butterflies
Curds
Girds
Utter lies

Pen to send
Lean and bend
Emote
Share
Words
Care

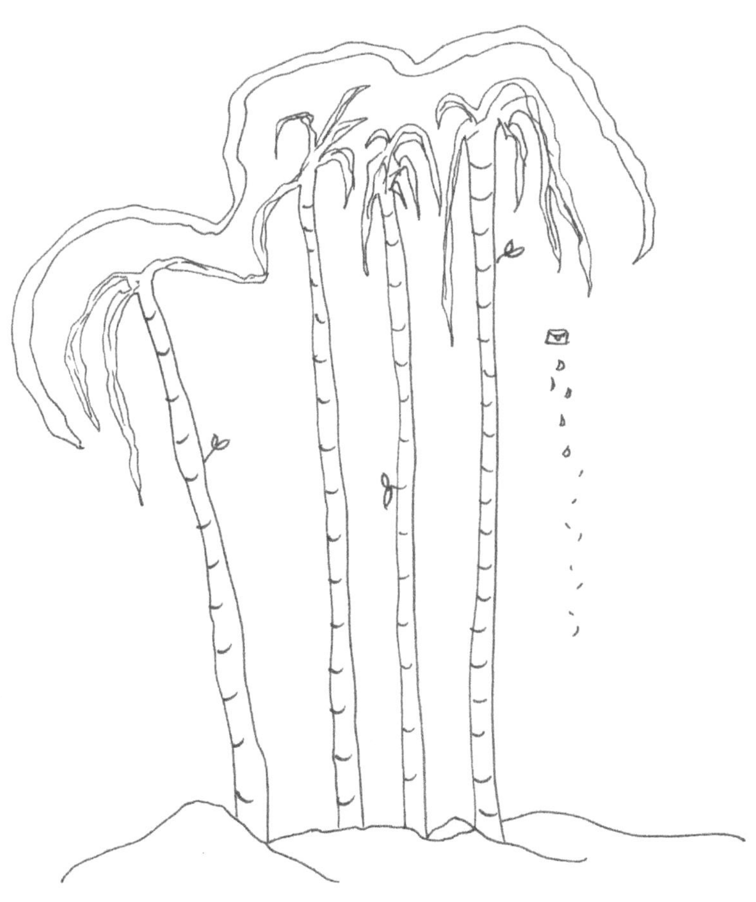

Passing Winds

The cosmic winter arrives
Through lifetimes
"I have been waiting," she says
You carried yourself to me
And I've carried you through
Lifetimes
Through passing winds

I could leave it all
The reasons I could
I can always change my mind

"No regrets"
It's best to say
You and I
We cannot stay
When will we be far away?

No talk of the end
Who, why or when
Who are we?
Let's not pretend

Shadows

If I knew in shadows made
Extended boundaries all but paid
Everything under the sun
Can be broken, split
Undone
Along the moonlit road we pass
Will love and light prevail at last?

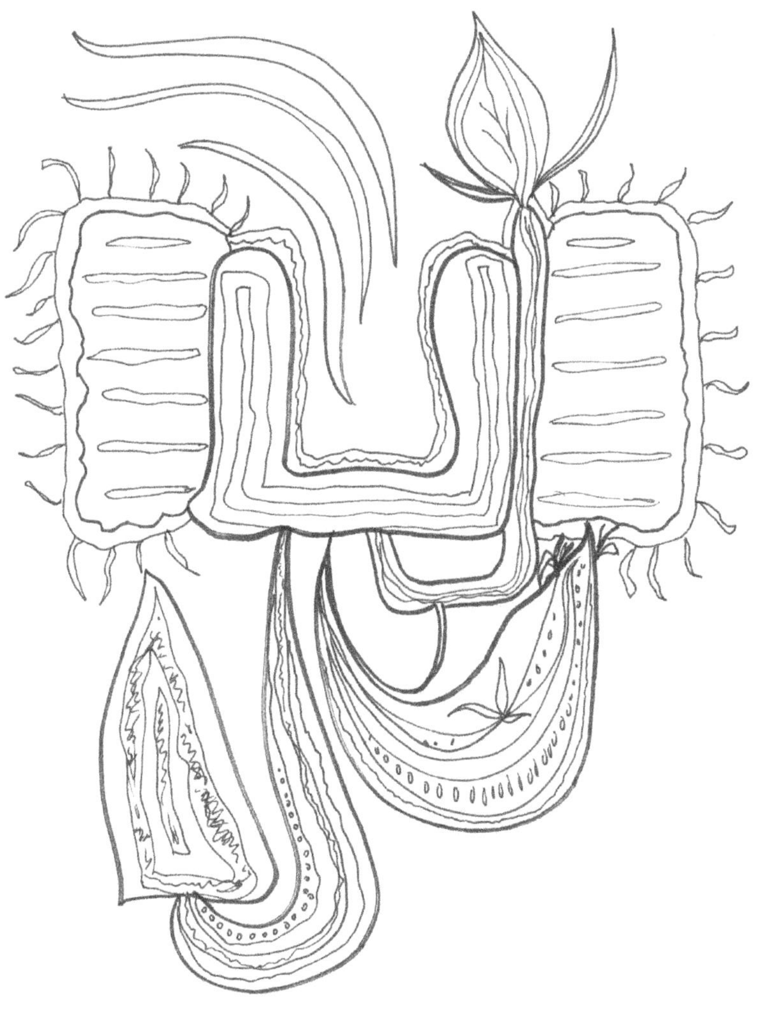

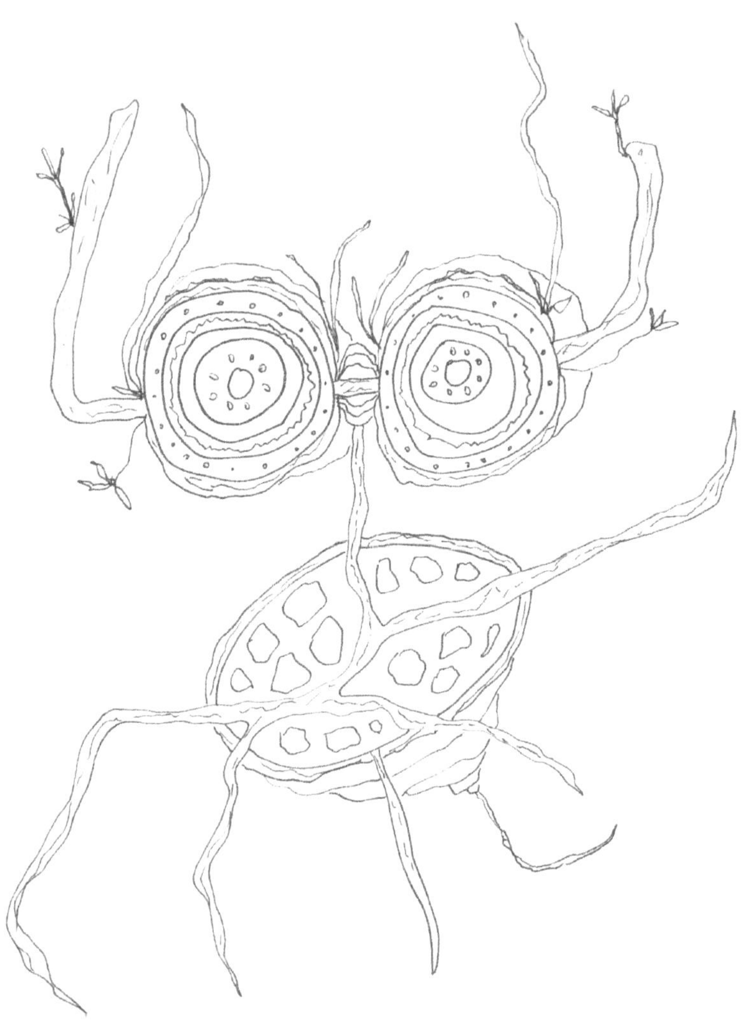

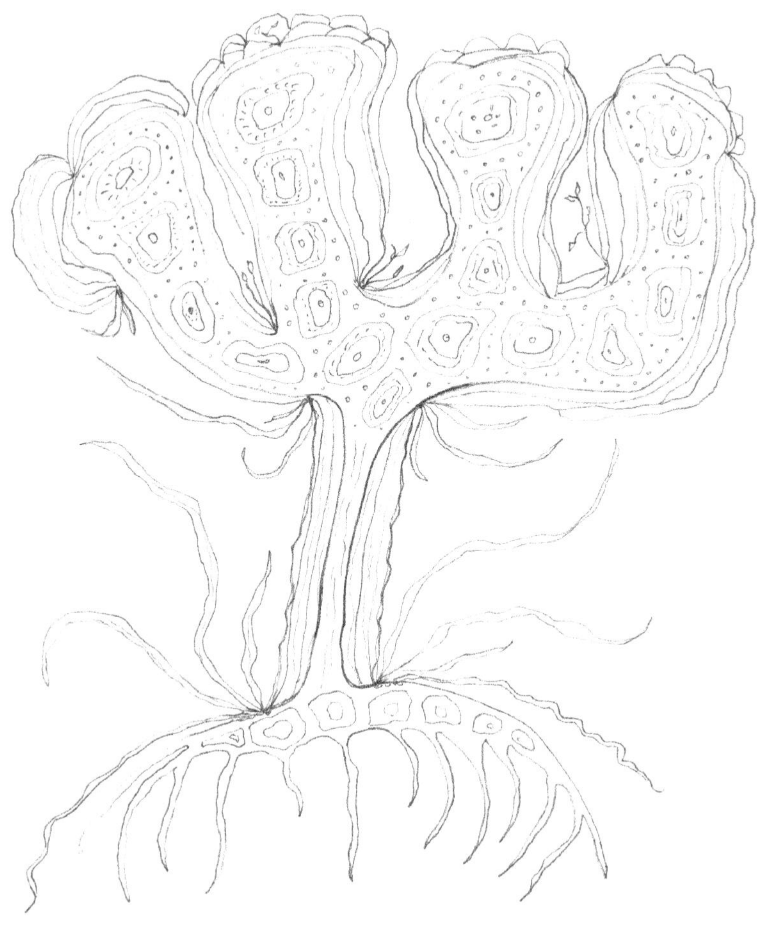

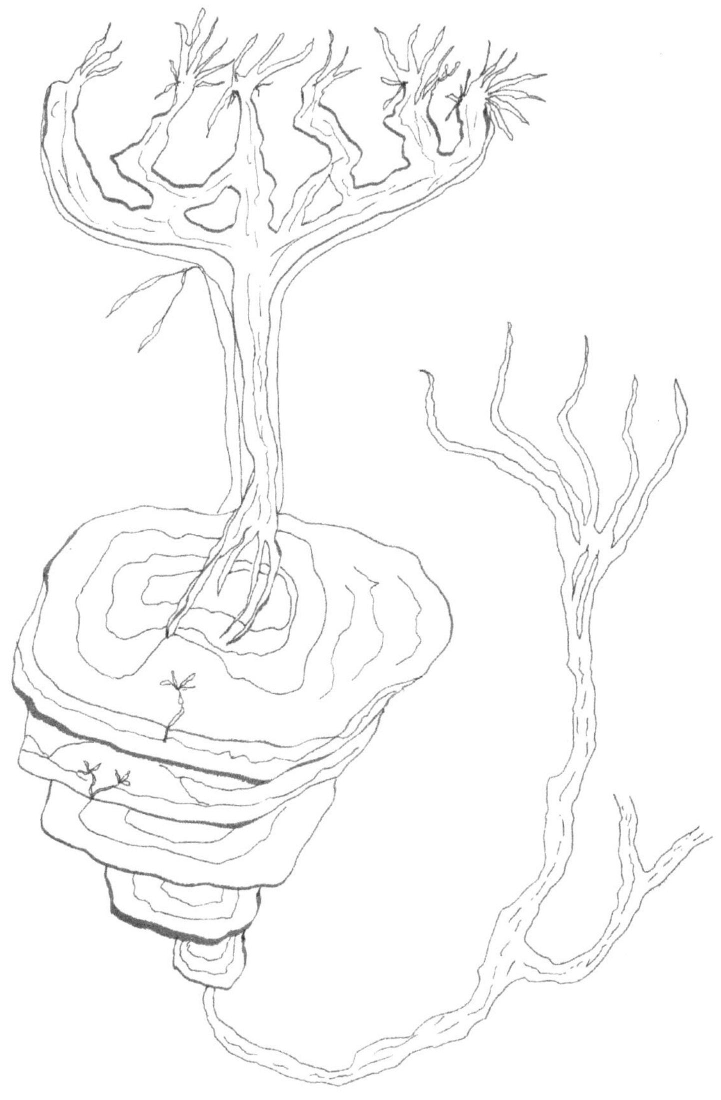

Temple guards
Formation
Around the light
Afraid to shine
Layers of dark and dark
And light
Mirrors of far and far
And wide
Dusk to dawn
The winter snow
Summer rain
Bitter glow
Fade, the shade
Cast below
Storms, the swarms
Nowhere to go
Tides will turn
Live and learn
Storms and swarms
Feel the burn

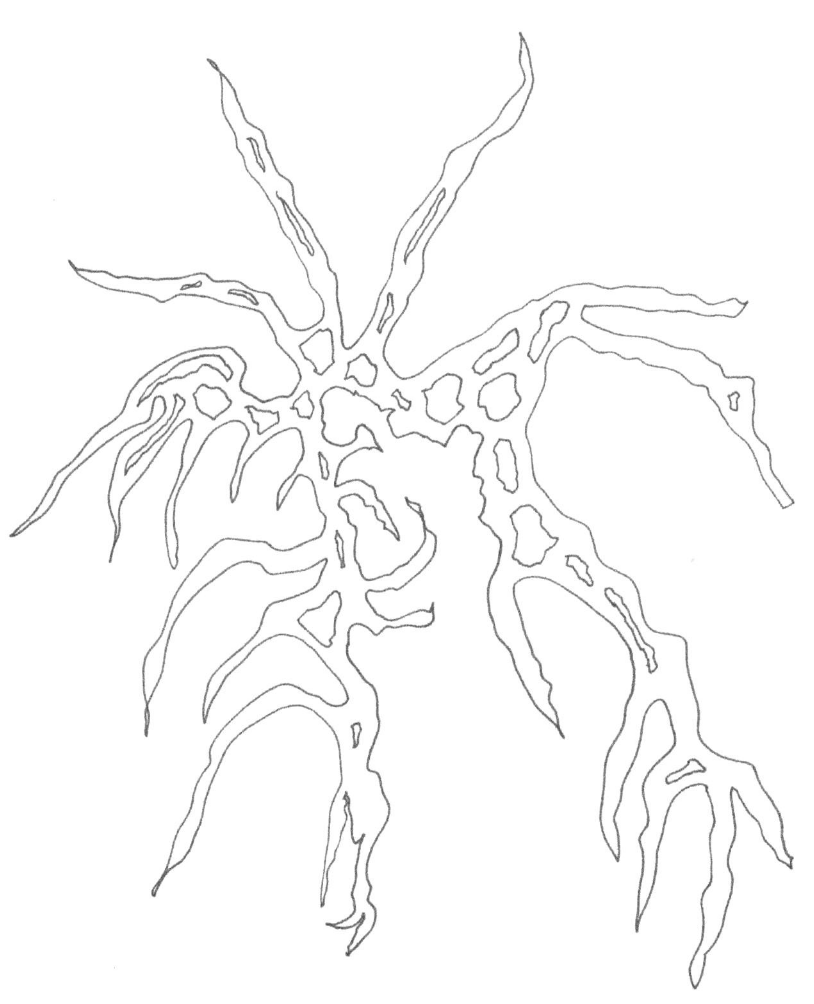

Control
B roll
Internet
Cigarette
Look
Shook
Make a
mess
Pressure
Stress
Down
Frown
Memorize
Crown
Brown
Agonize

Wish
Kiss
Miss
Diss
Fight
Bite
Hate
Bait

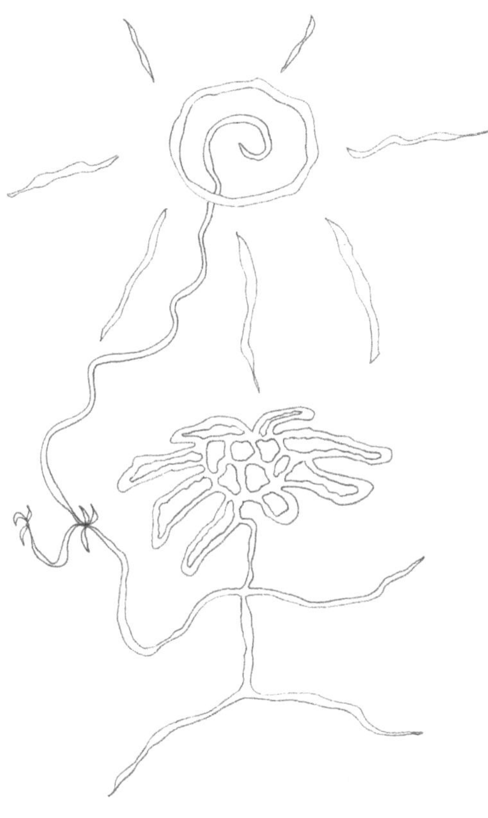

Stop
Drop
Look in
Look up
Reach out
Reach up
Create
Emanate
Educate
Ruminate
Contemplate
Meditate
Integrate
Celebrate

Control
B roll
Be the lead
Plant the seed

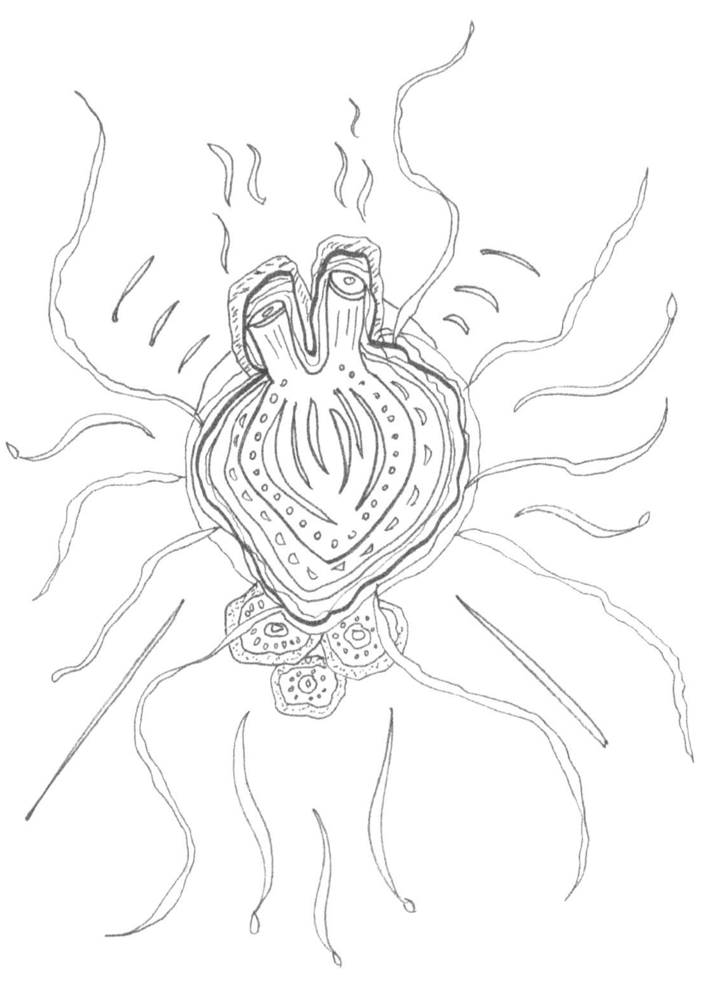

Will you ever change?
Could life rearrange
To recreate
And separate
The hurtful stain?

The time has changed
Gone against the grain
To serenade
And heal the pain

Will they ever change?
Their lies have quite the range
Hard not to get enraged
Can't make a person change

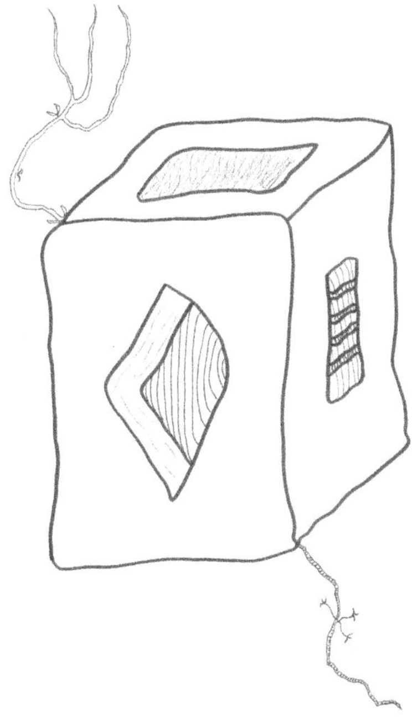

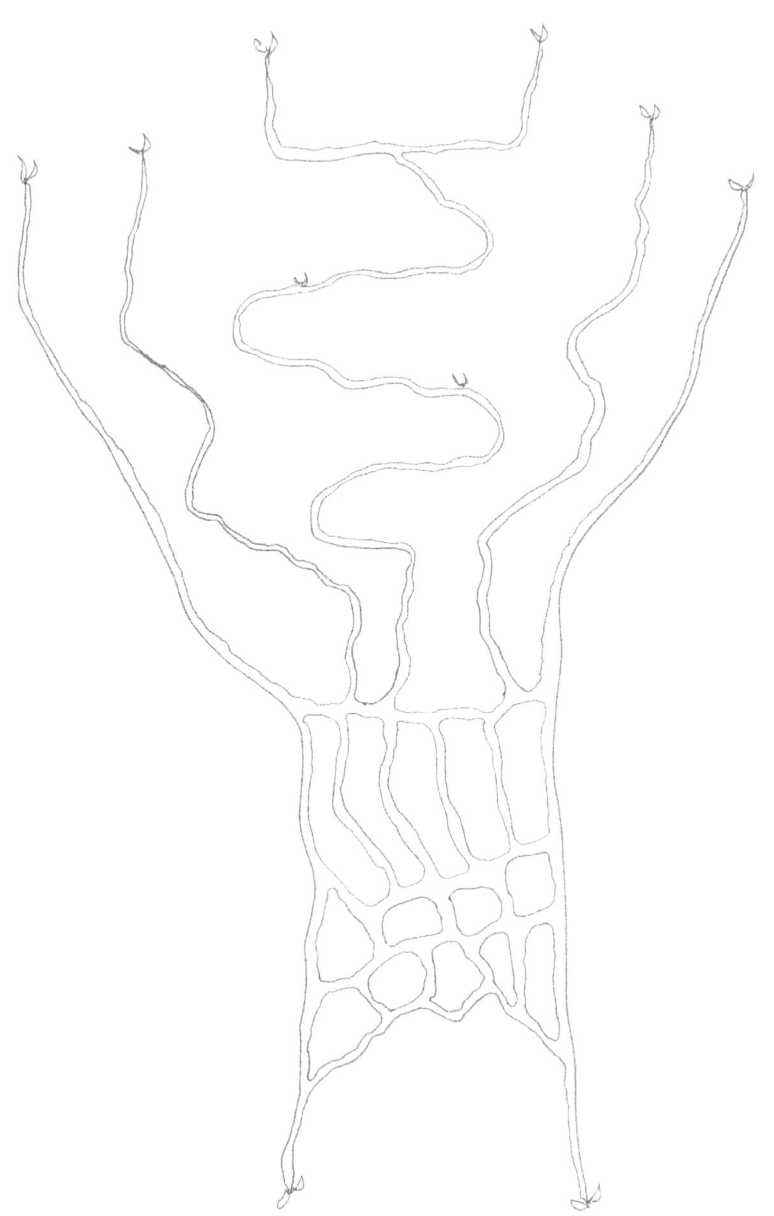

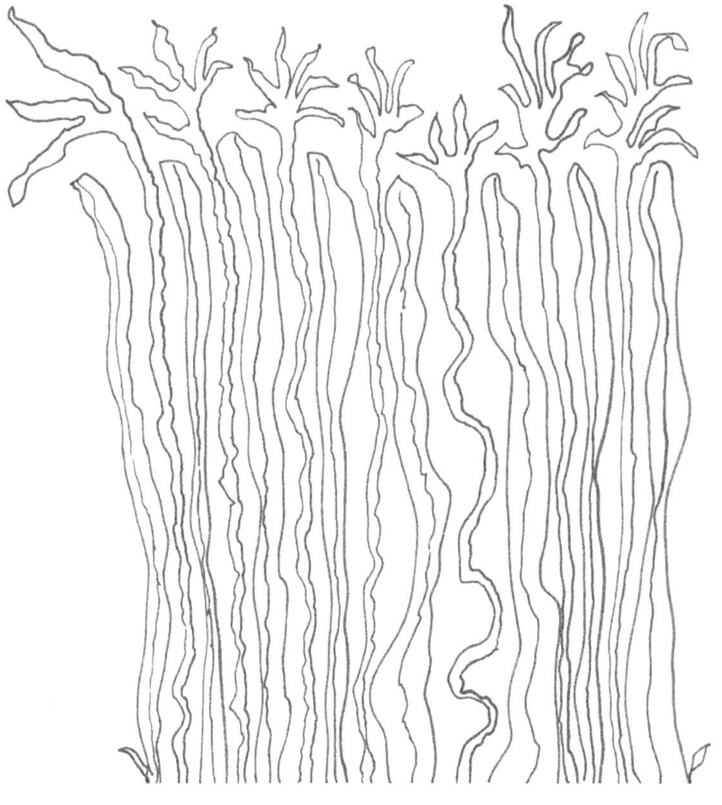

I wonder how they sleep at night
While here I lay
Stone cold in fright
Pinch and grab
Hurt some more
Flip the ceiling and the floor
Close your eyes and do this now
Someone else will wipe your brow
Time and time and time again
Close to me
You're not my friend
Closer still
And play pretend
Pain that may not ever end
Molded by a parasite
Laying cold
Still in fright
Vision blinded
Clouded sight
Holding
Searching
For the Light

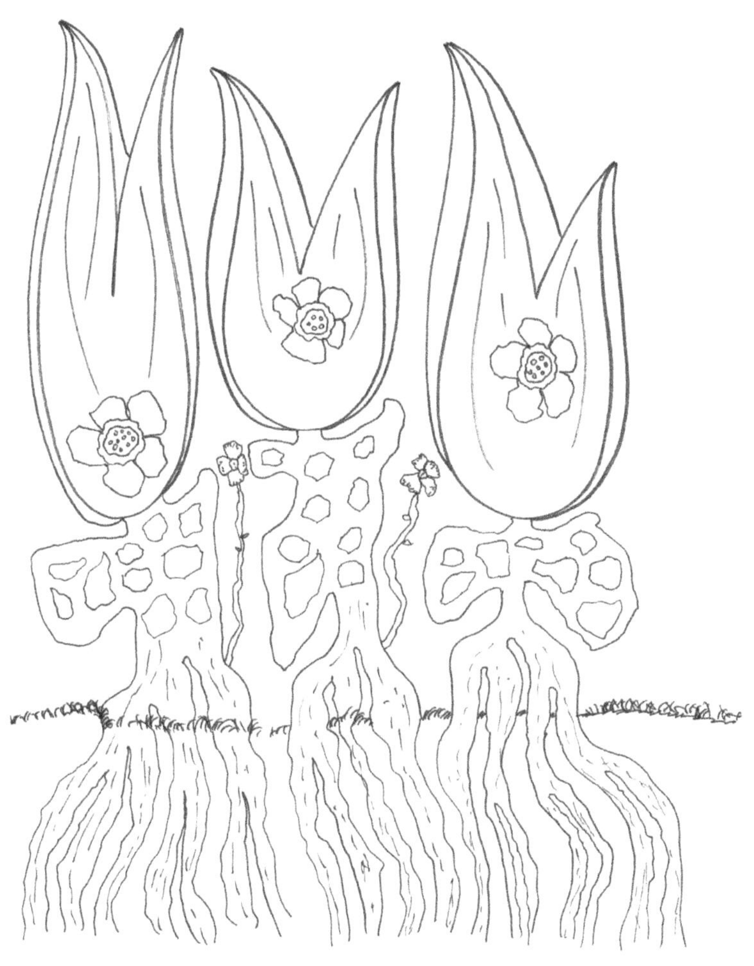

Walking through the mud
Through the thick of it
Time has ways to make a day
Big and small at the same time

Miracles
Cures
Fixes
Sorries relieve
The burning itches
Temperamental madres
Glorious queens
A walk through the fire
For no one else
But me

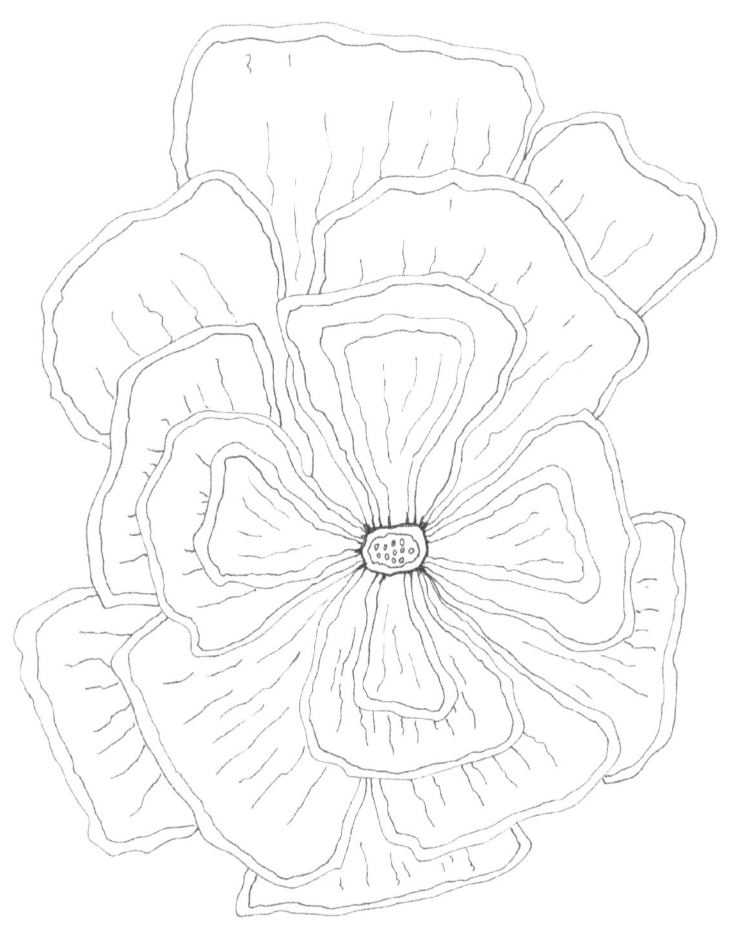

Sink
Swim
Lose
Win
Hold the light

Cruise
Bruise
Reason
Treason
Hold the light

Sickness
Weakness
Bigness
Meekness
Hold the light

Carry
Marry
Listen
Glisten
Hold the light

Little girl in a red dress
Stay wide awake
Little girl in the red dress
Please don't be late
The tide's always turning
And the wheels still go 'round
Little girl in the red dress
You're safe and sound

Little one in a blue coat
Color of your life
Little one in a blue coat
Follow your light
The sun always rises
And the moon shines at night
Little one in a blue coat
Keep hope in sight

Little girl in a raincoat
Stay on that smile
Little girl in a raincoat
Shining so bright
The sun always rises
And the moon shines at night
Little girl in a raincoat
Follow your light

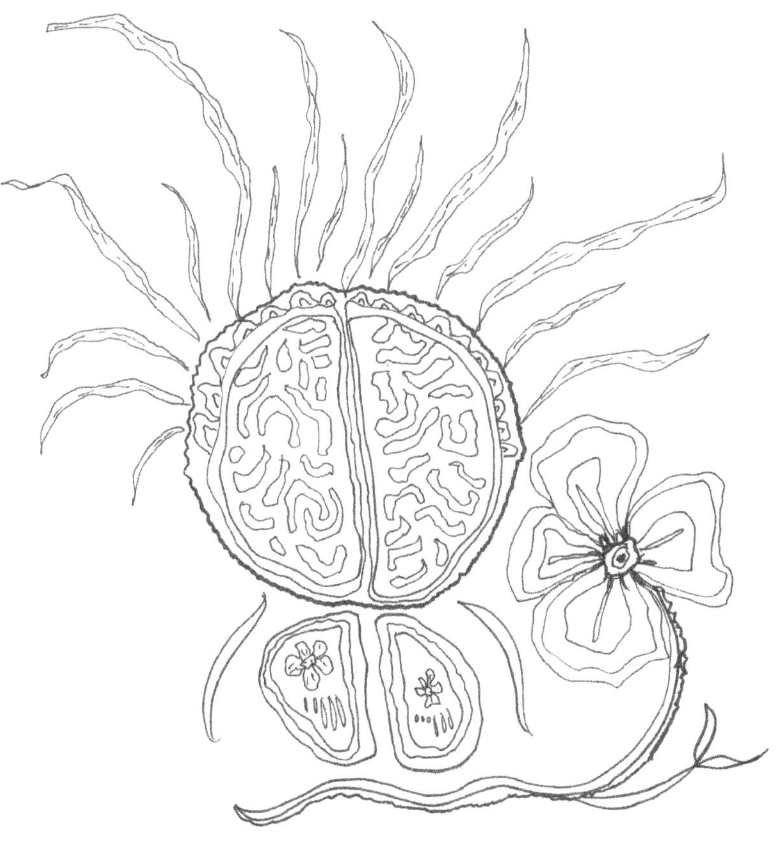

Empty walls
Empty staircase
Empty suitcase
Empty halls

Why can't I be empty?

Empty banquet
Empty feast
Not an ordinary beast

Why can't I be empty?

Empty sound
Empty note
Every passage that I wrote
Clouded visions
Tough decisions

Why can't I be empty?

Empty pocket
Empty socket
Something written in the docket

Why can't I be empty?

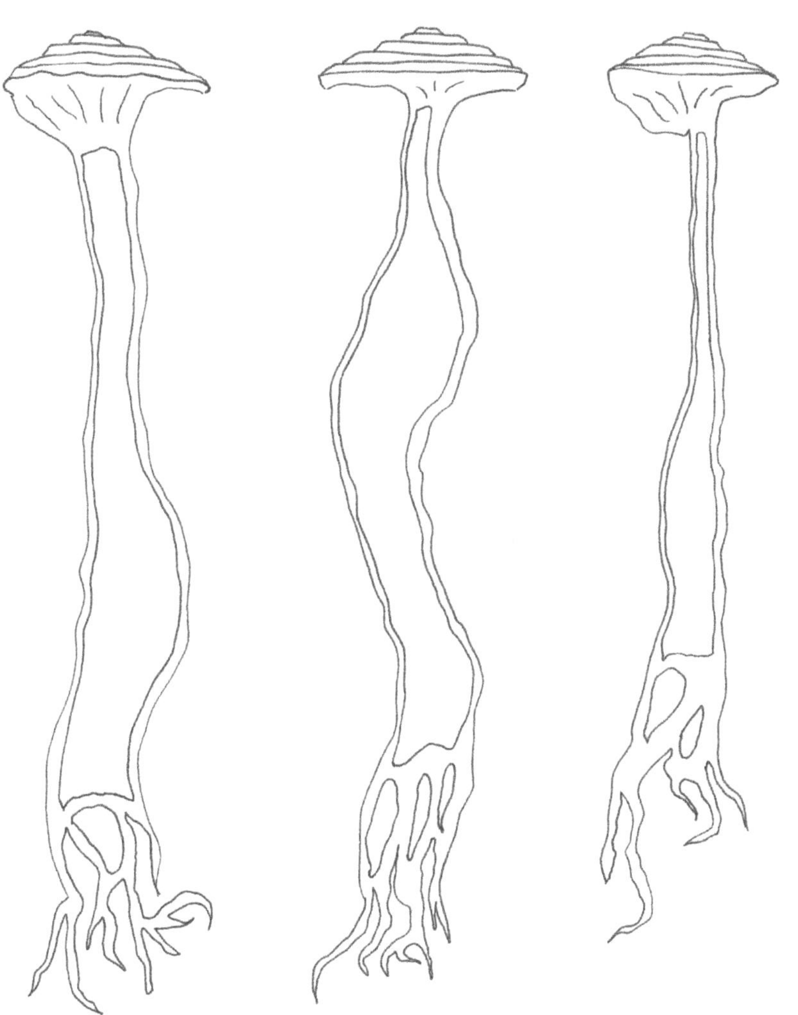

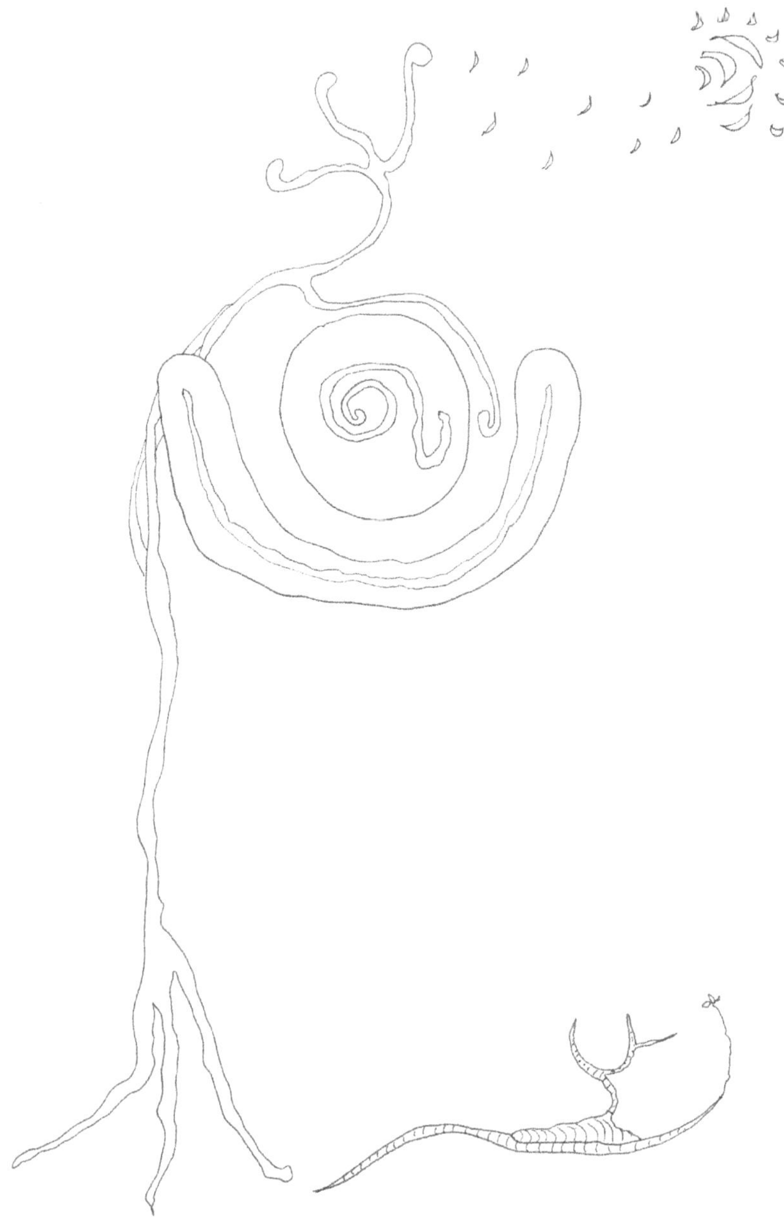

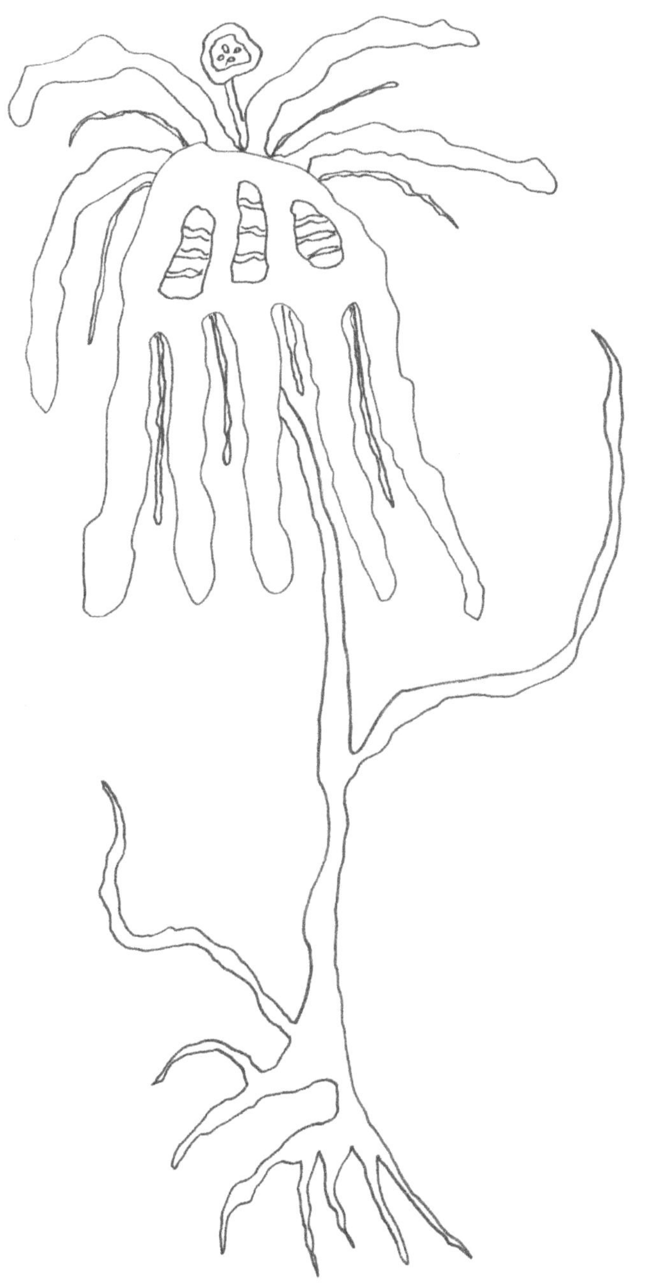

Why are you hiding
If you're not lying
Why do you run
If you're soaking in the sun
Why do you laugh
When young strangers pass
Why do need
To force and feed
Why do you bother
Telling mother and father
Why do you leave
If we're to believe
You have no degree
Of causing disease
Why do you smile
At something so vile

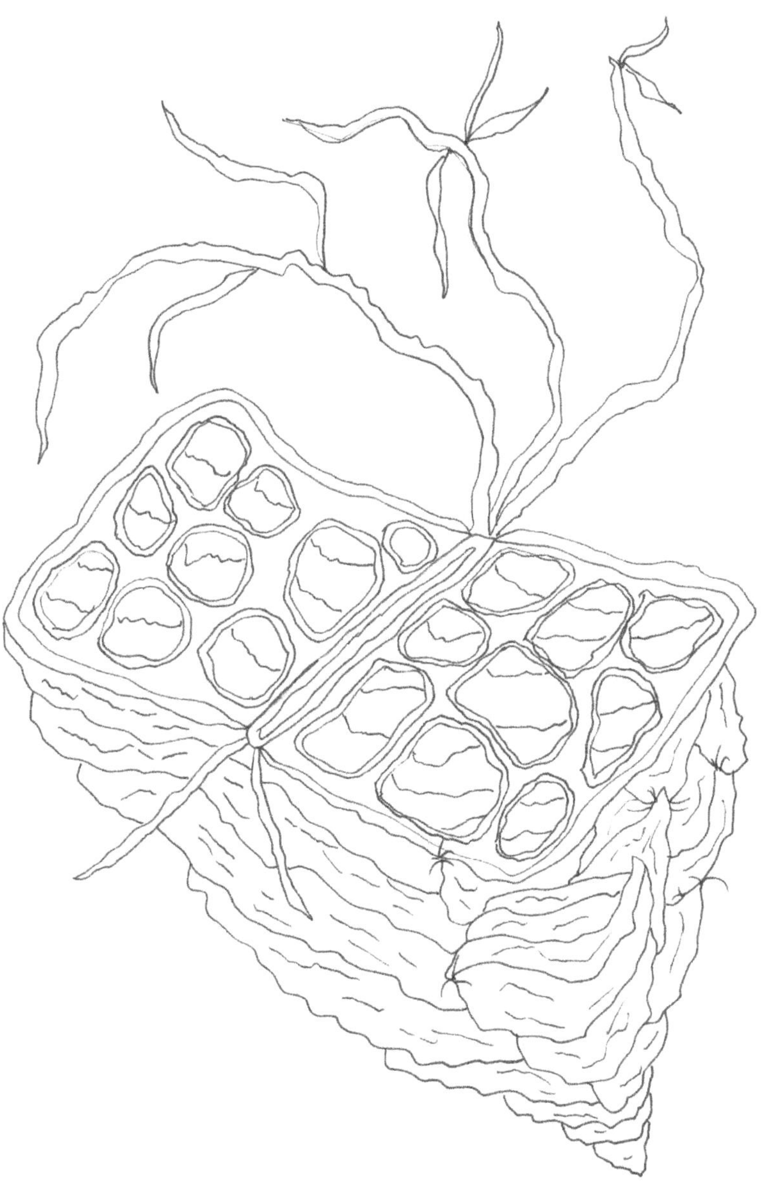

One day
I'll see my friends
In New York

    Someday
    I'll see my friends
    In Chicago

        One day
        I'll see my friends
        In the Philippines

            Someday
            I'll see my friends
            In L.A.

One day
I'll see my friends
At the restaurant

    Someday
    I'll see my friends
    At the park

        One day
        I'll see my friends
        At the banquet hall

            Someday
            I'll see my friends
            At the mall

One day
I'll see my friends
At the matinee

    Someday
    I'll see my friends
    At the pier

        One day
        I'll see my friends
        On the mountain top

            Someday
            I'll see my friends
            Without fear

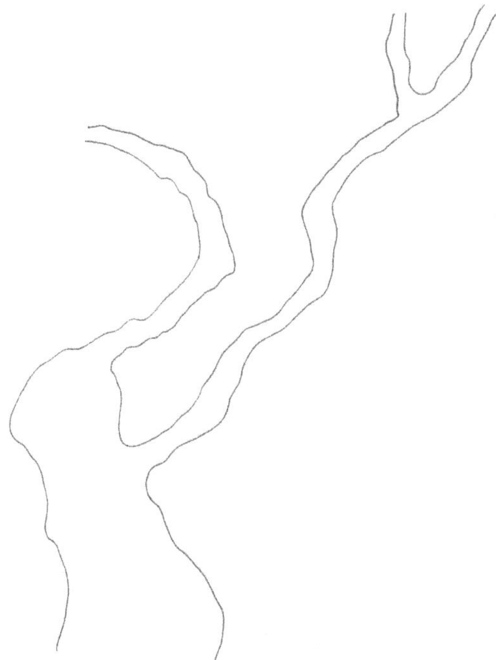

Choosing Life

You can't take my life with you
You can't break my light
You can turn away
And face the truth
To back my youth
I live my life
I'll live my life

I live on
From now on
My beauty shines
My heart, my mind
True love within
God's intention
My choice
My life
My own invention
Only now
No past
Just present
Here today
Living heaven

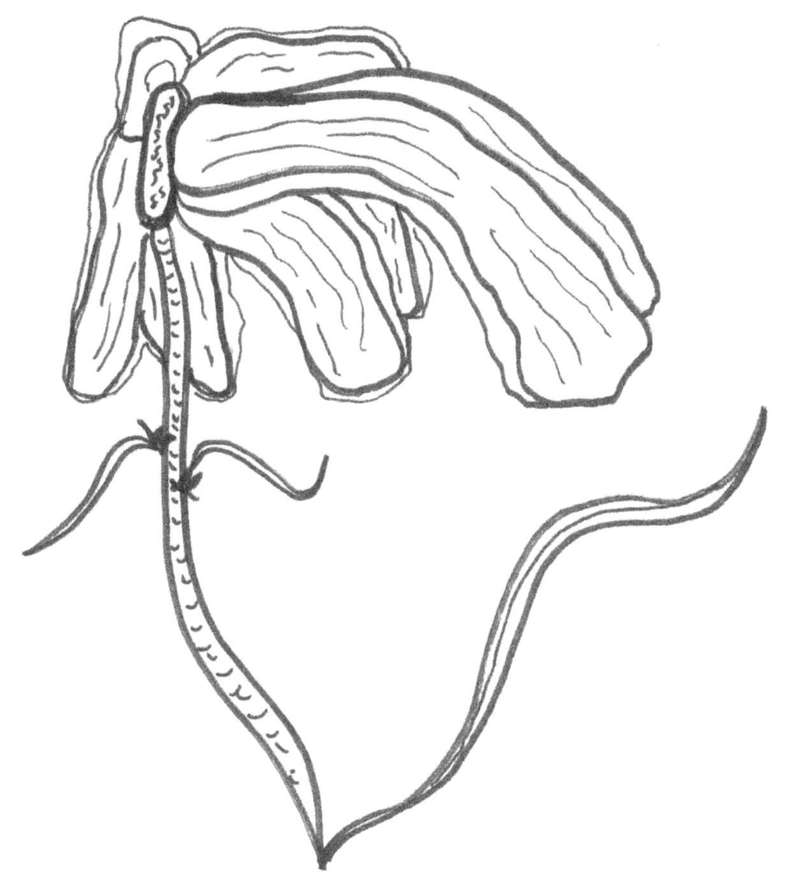

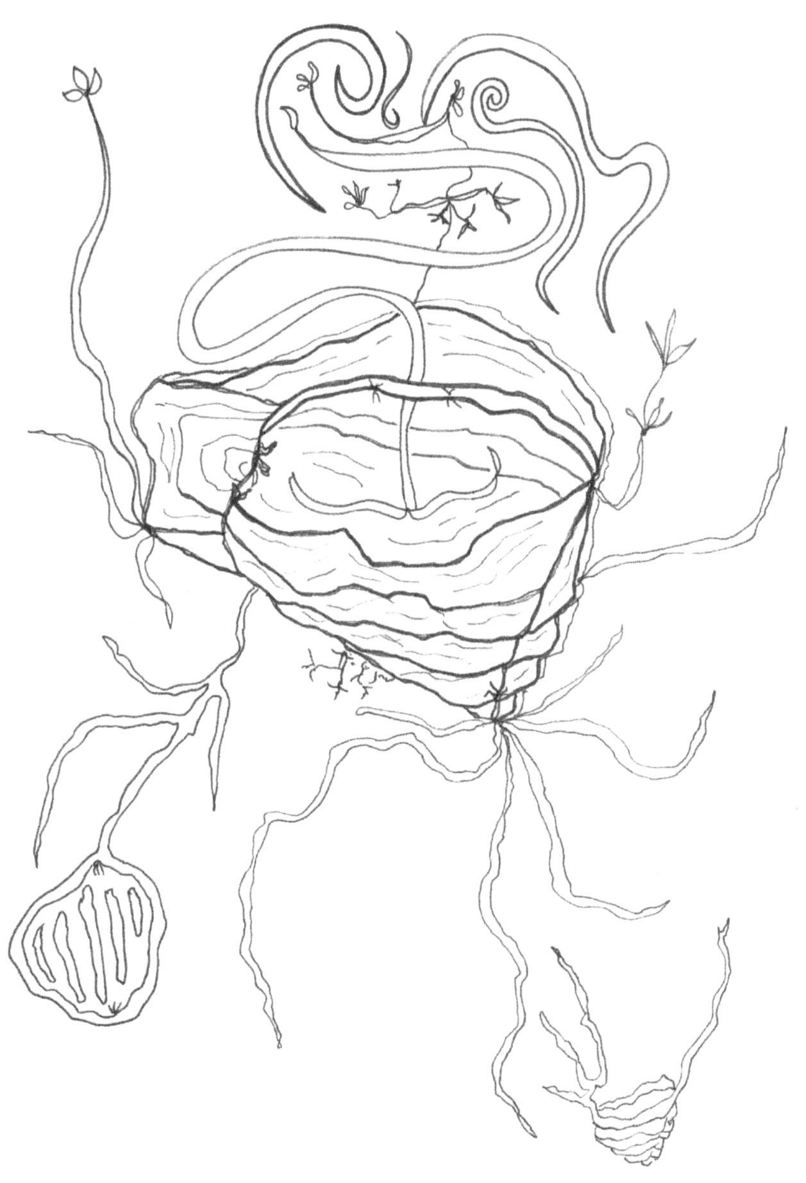

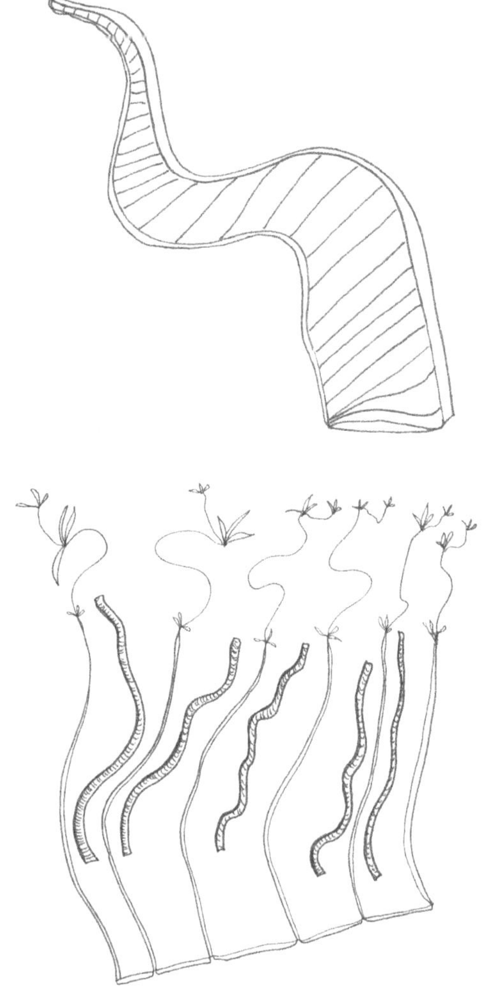

Oh, you play?
Faceless face
Empty space
Void of grace

Left from right
Notes by sight
Compared to who
What do you do
Band of judges
Ink without smudges
Prove to myself
No one else
Sanctity
For mind and health

Weightless
Gracious
Deserved esteem
Lightness
Brightness
Realized dream
Timeless
Boundless
Evergreen

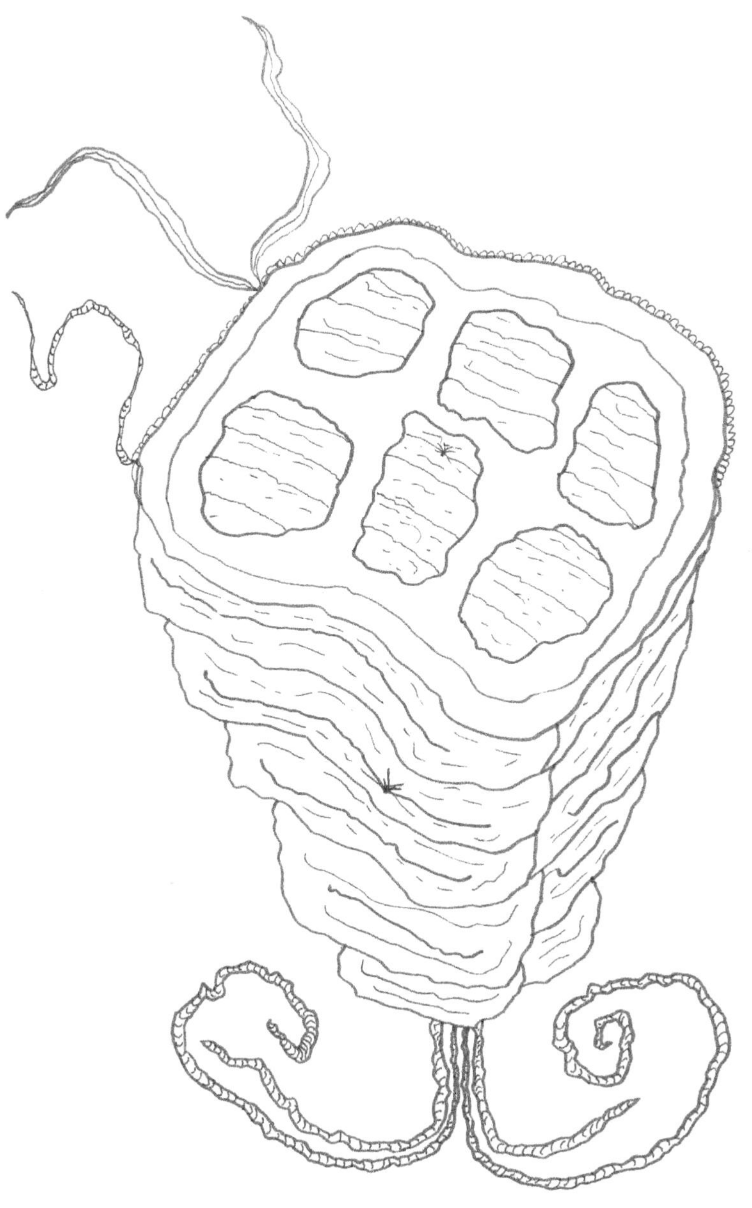

Lies
Alibis
Children cry
Don't ask why
Blackened sky
No dry eye
Testify
Amplify
Clarify
Signify

I won't ask why
I'll never know
Why ice can melt
The winter snow
Revealing sickness
Devoid of reason
Festering, blistering
Season by season

I won't ask why
The clouds fly by
Stirring shadows
Smoke and ashes
Covering a thirsty soil
Thunder screaming
Living things quivering

I won't ask why
What's seen through eyes
Elaborate disguise
For power and might
For pleasure and pain
The story remains
I speculate
What you create

I won't ask why
You live in lies
In plain deceit
Four walls
Concrete
Bars and jars
Jacket straight
Where's the soul
To liberate

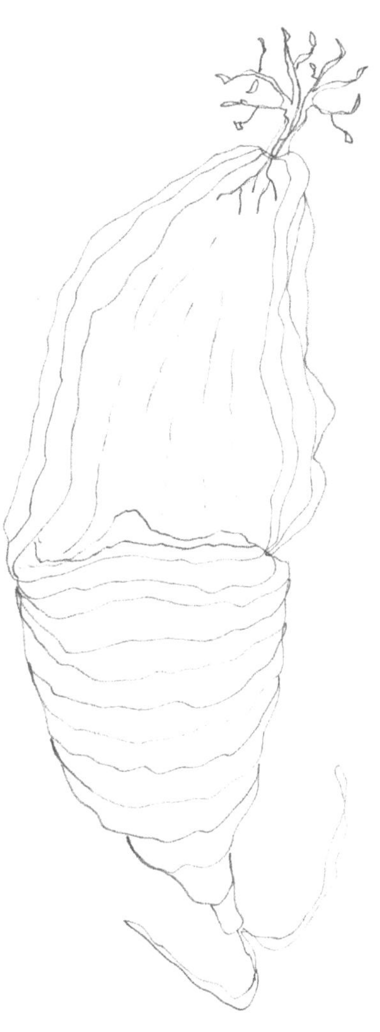

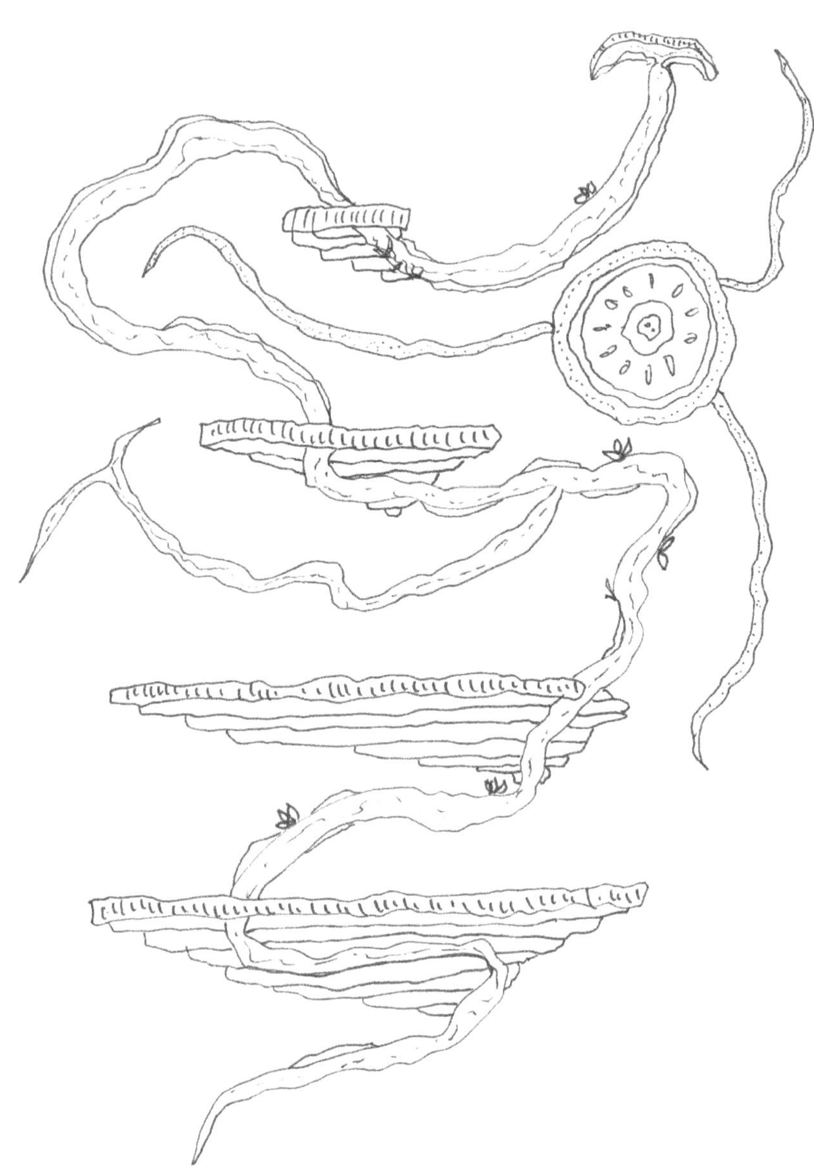

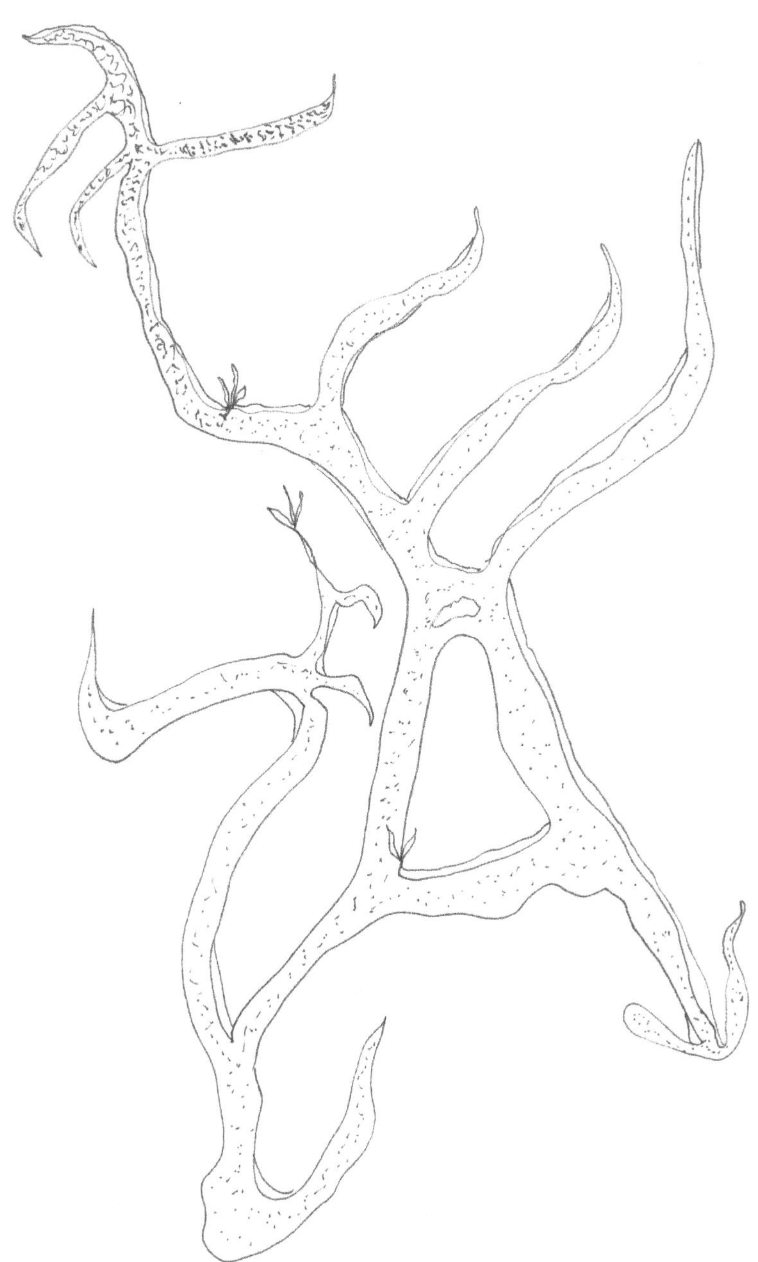

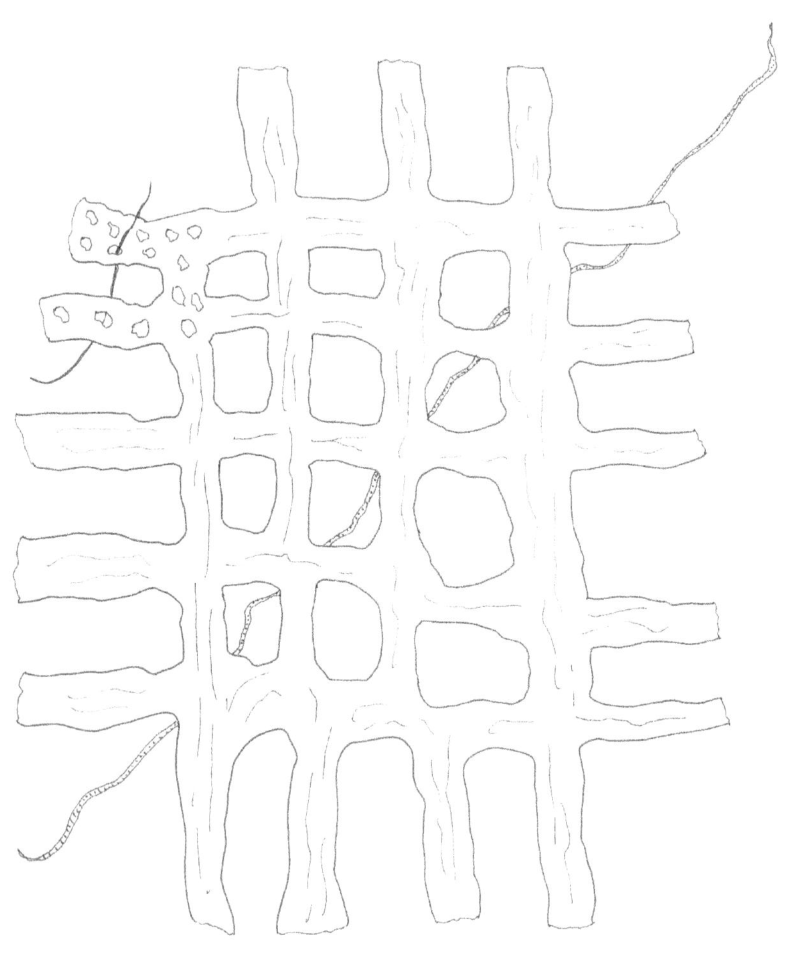

Stones Cast

Faster cast to dodge the past
Stones and rocks that never last
Scheming, gleaning, nasty tasks
A question that is never asked

What rooted hate arriving late
Hurry, worry, endure and wait
Wounded once again, again
A feeling that just wants to end

Take and take and take once more
Take until it hits the floor
Break the evil to the core
Break into the cracking door

Fade to dust and float in space
Where no one else can see that face
No teeth, no bones, no dwelling place
An ugly, shattered fall from grace

No more to blend and permeate
To turn to move and twist the fate
At last the heart will emanate
A light to shine and celebrate

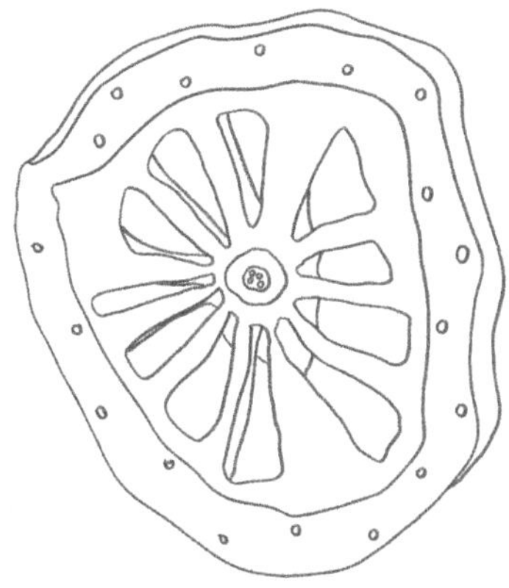

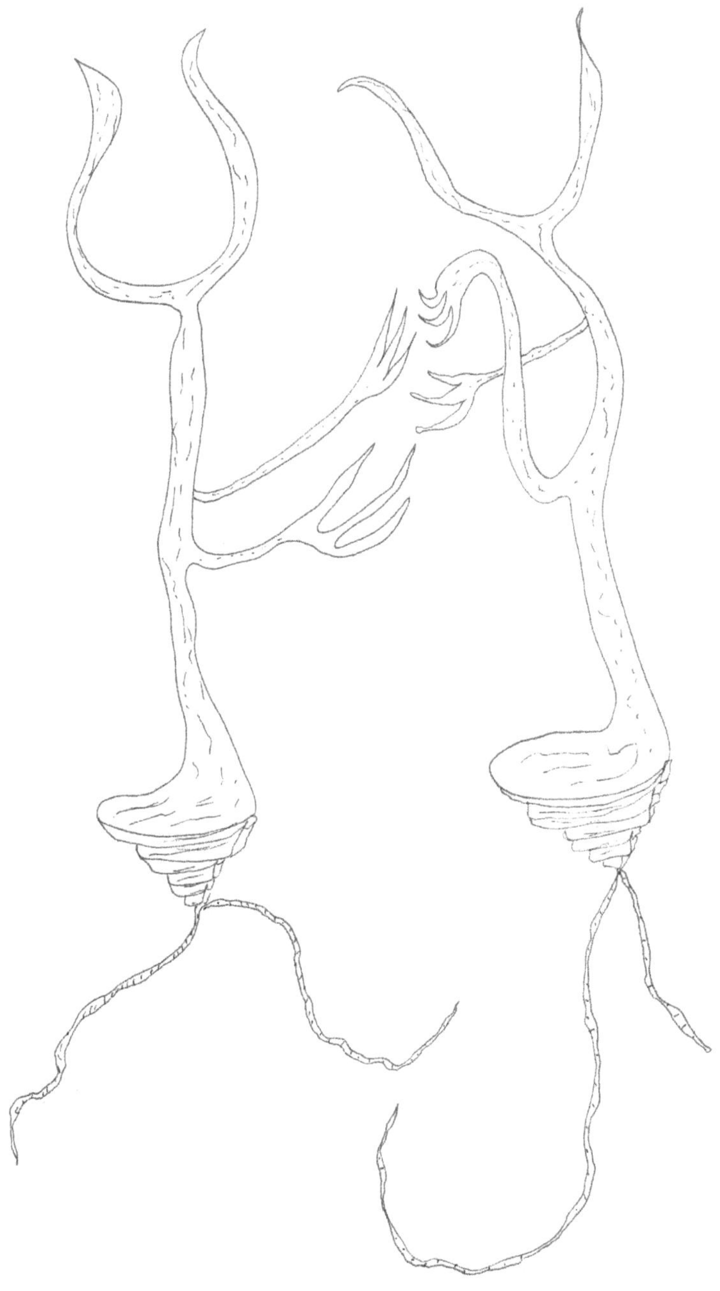

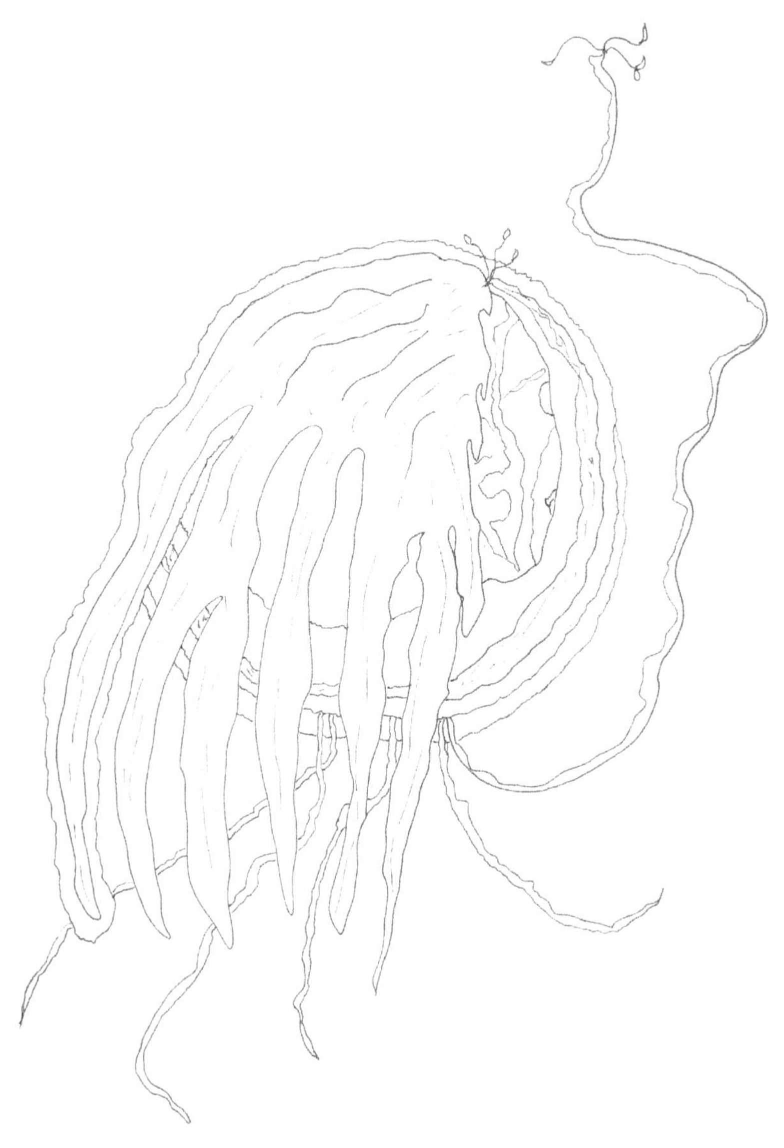

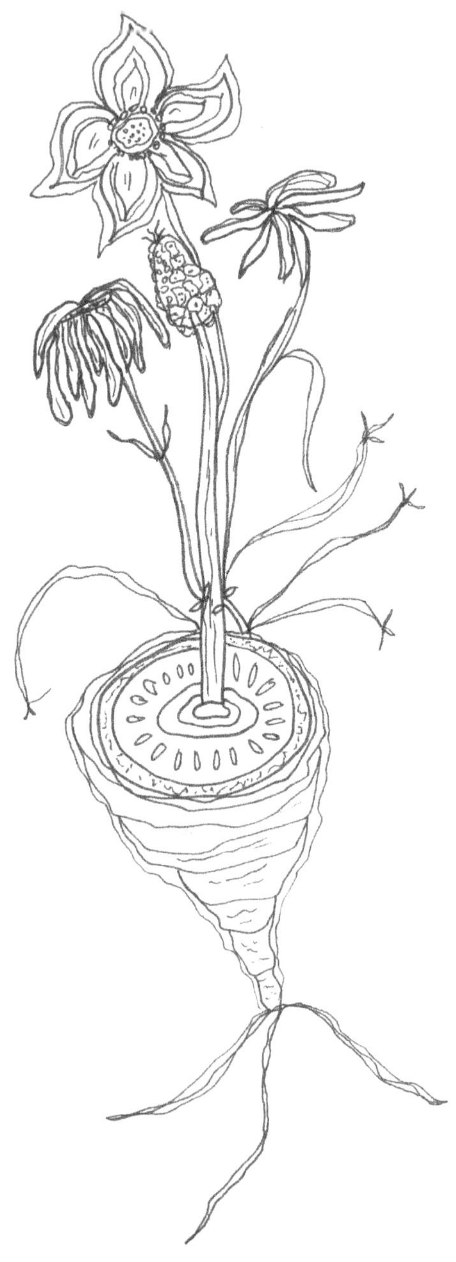

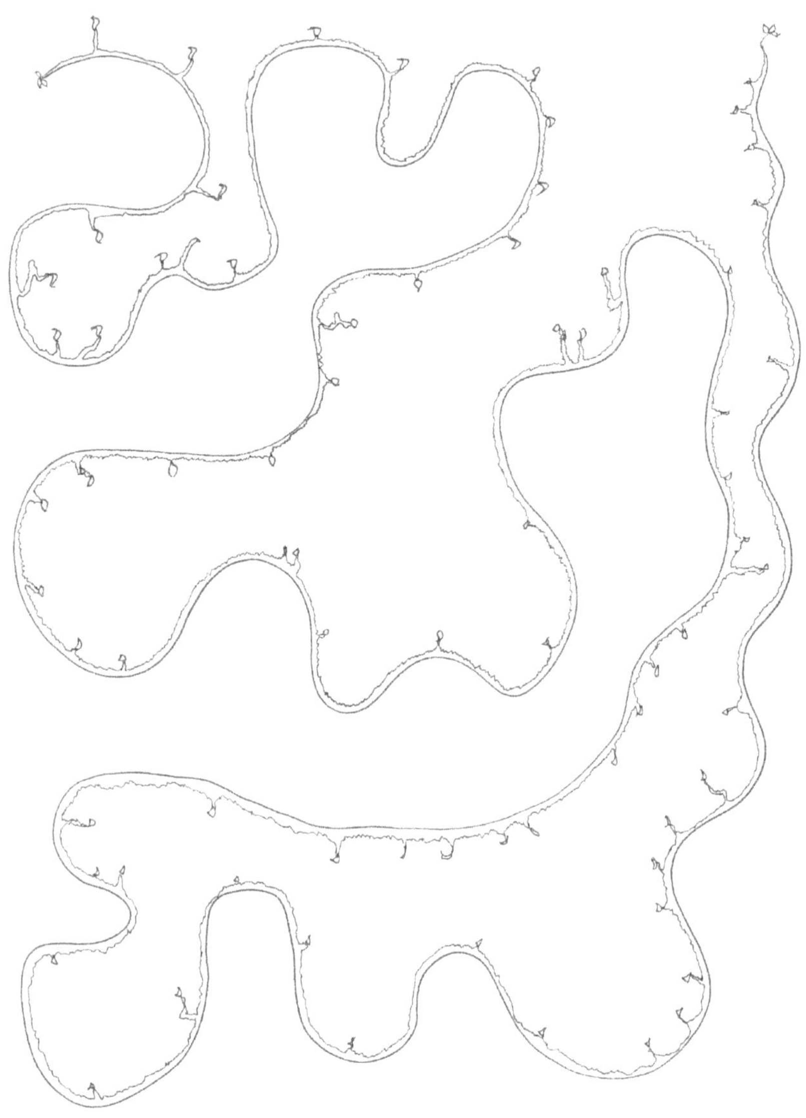

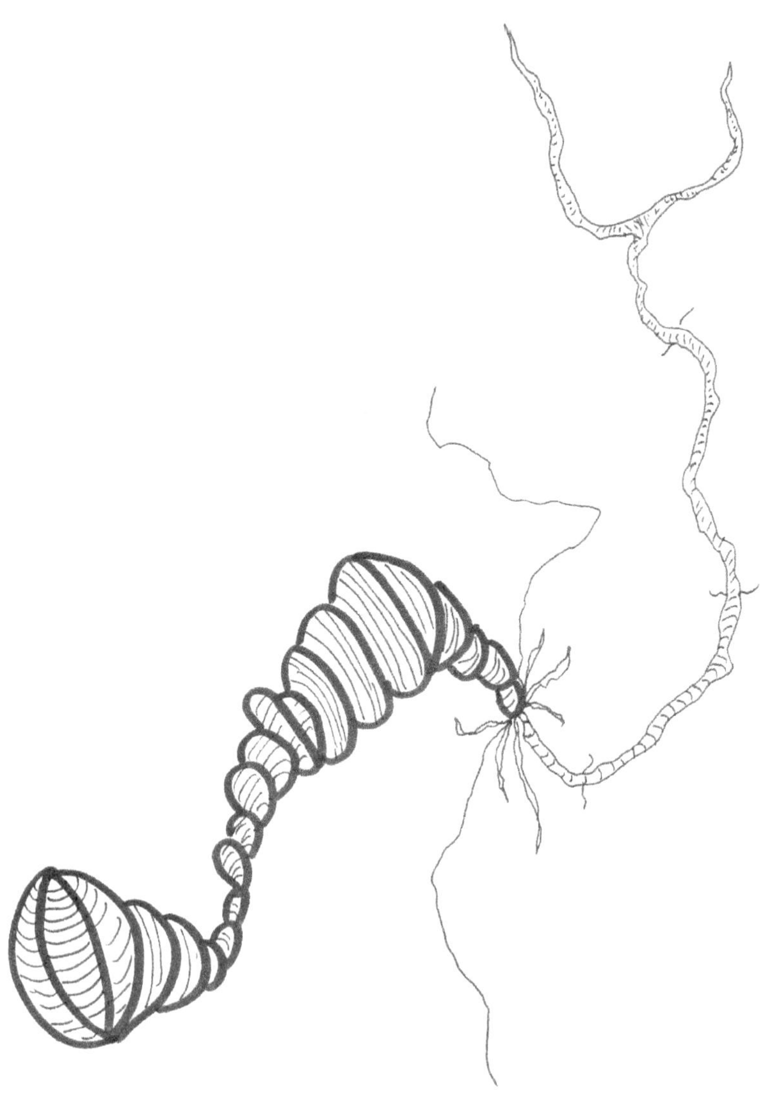

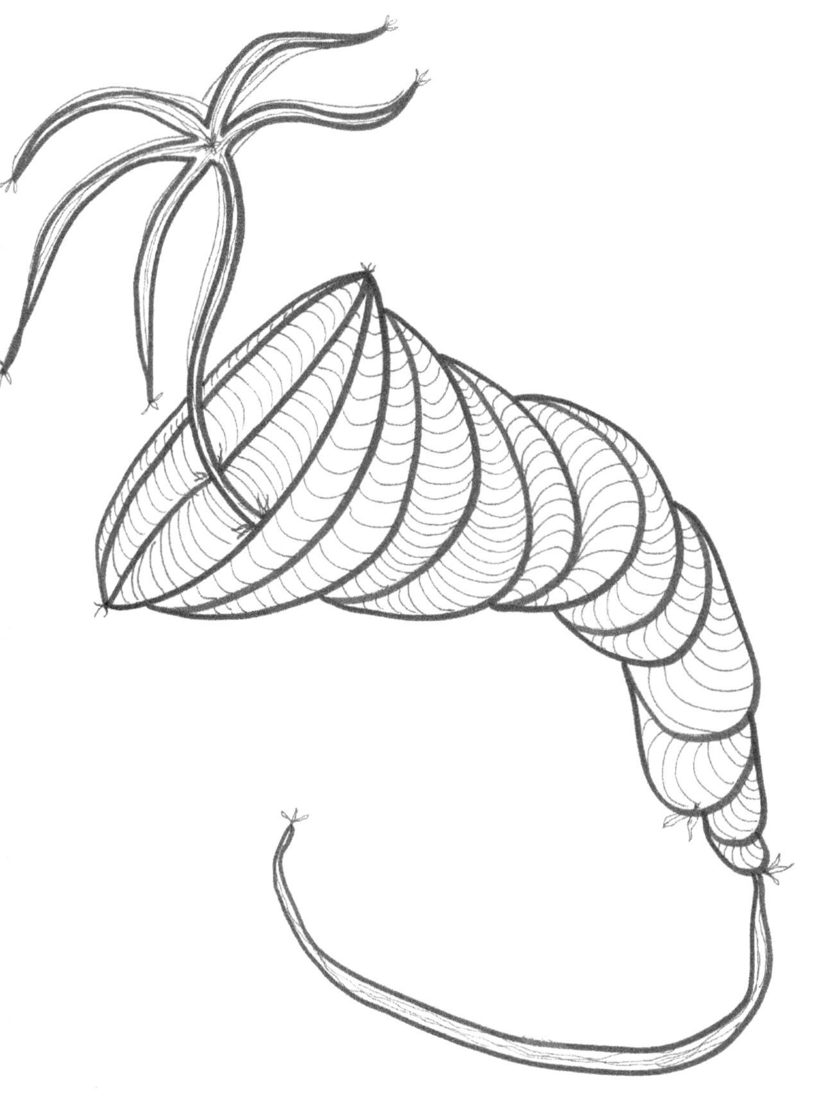

As softly as the rain falls
As quietly as the wind blows
The steady hand will guide
Inside the child's mind
If sorrow passes
Tomorrow higher
If sanded woods hold strong fire
Missed instances and narrow ways
Will say its time revealing days
Send a letter from above
Where hearts soar
And love is just
Make heavens
Perfect place
For me
Celestial eyes
See skies and sea

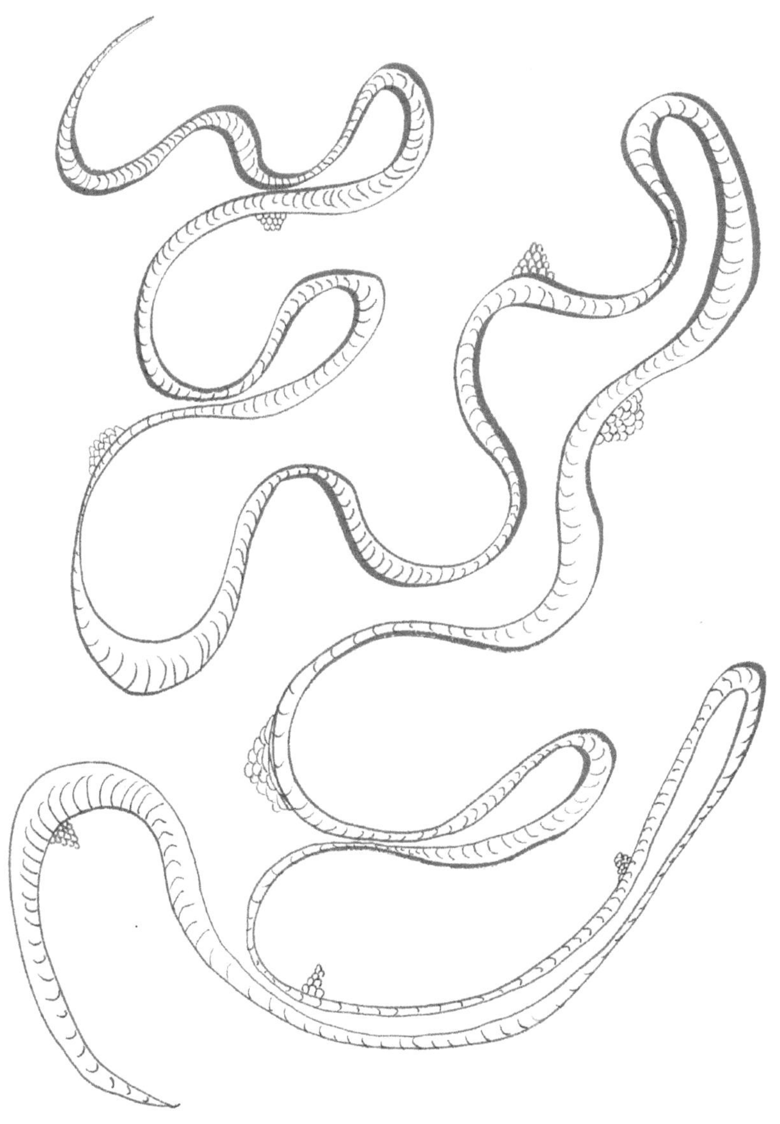

Self

Spring
Summer
Winter
Fall
Will I feel this way for all?
Every season to withdraw
Find what's written in the law

Monday
Tuesday
Saturday
Could there be another way?
Leaves turn brown
Sky turns blue
One more paper left to do

2030
2040
2050
And beyond
Here to strengthen every bond
See the masterpiece of life
Be a gentle, loving wife

Fifty
Sixty
Seventy
Flying through eternity
See through you and see through me
The love of self where we are free

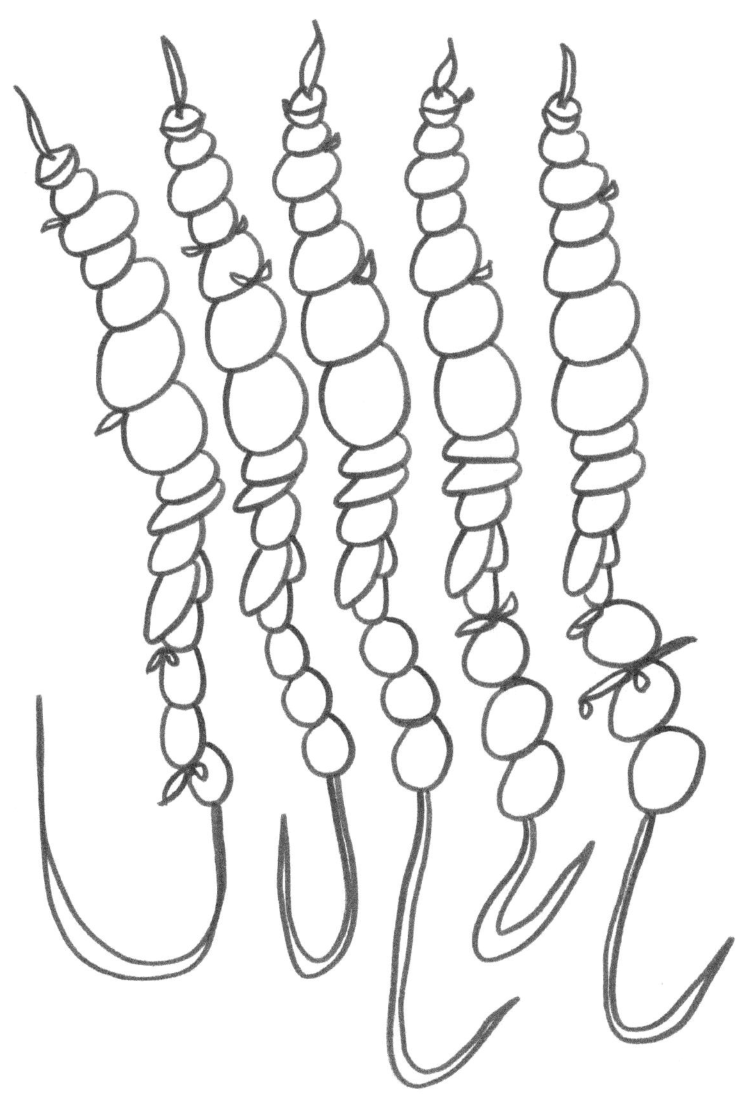

I was here yesterday
I am here today
Tomorrow is another day

You were here yesterday
You are here today
Tomorrow is another day

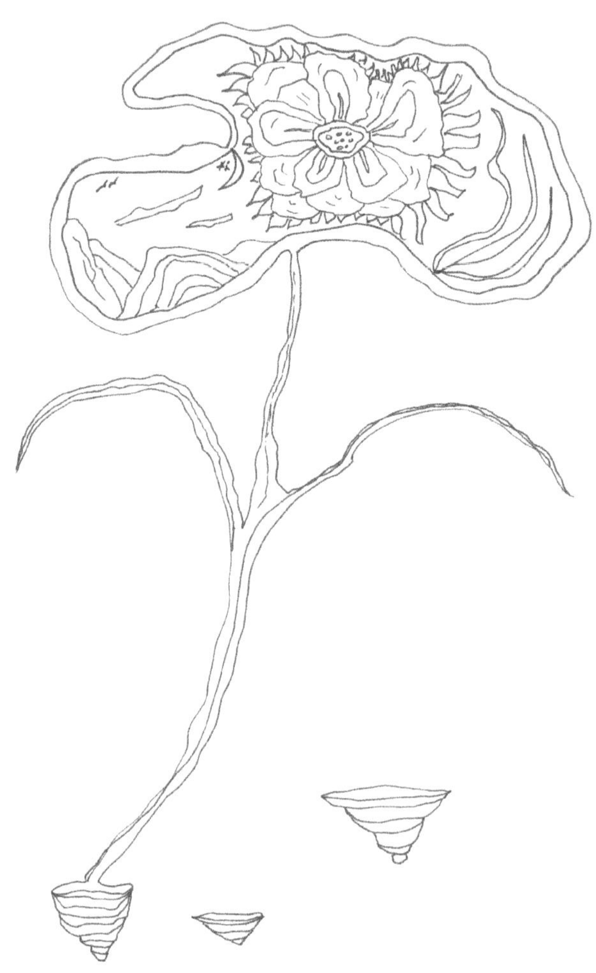

Turn the page
Blank slate
Blot the ink
Sign on the line
Show the team
Send it out
Pair them up
Elaborate
Commemorate
Share with care
Breathe the air
Walk the path
Tow the line
Hold the course
Have a ball
Get it done
Savor the flavor
See their eyes
Feel the vibe
Come alive
Smile inside
Surf the tide
Enjoy the ride

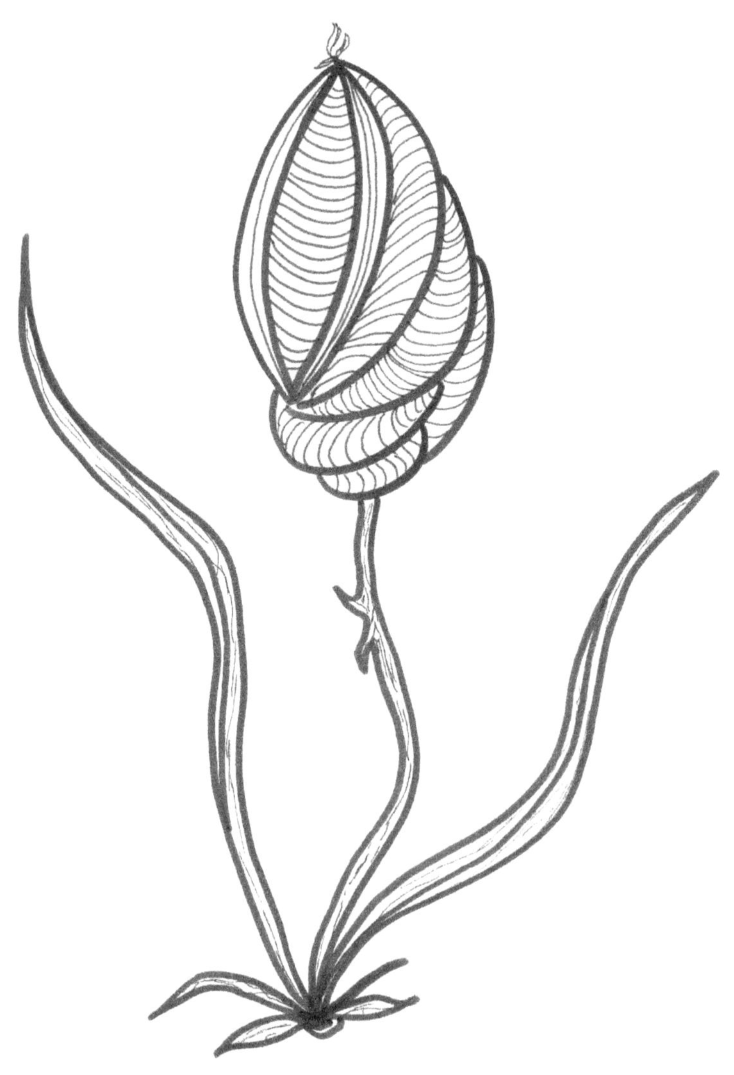

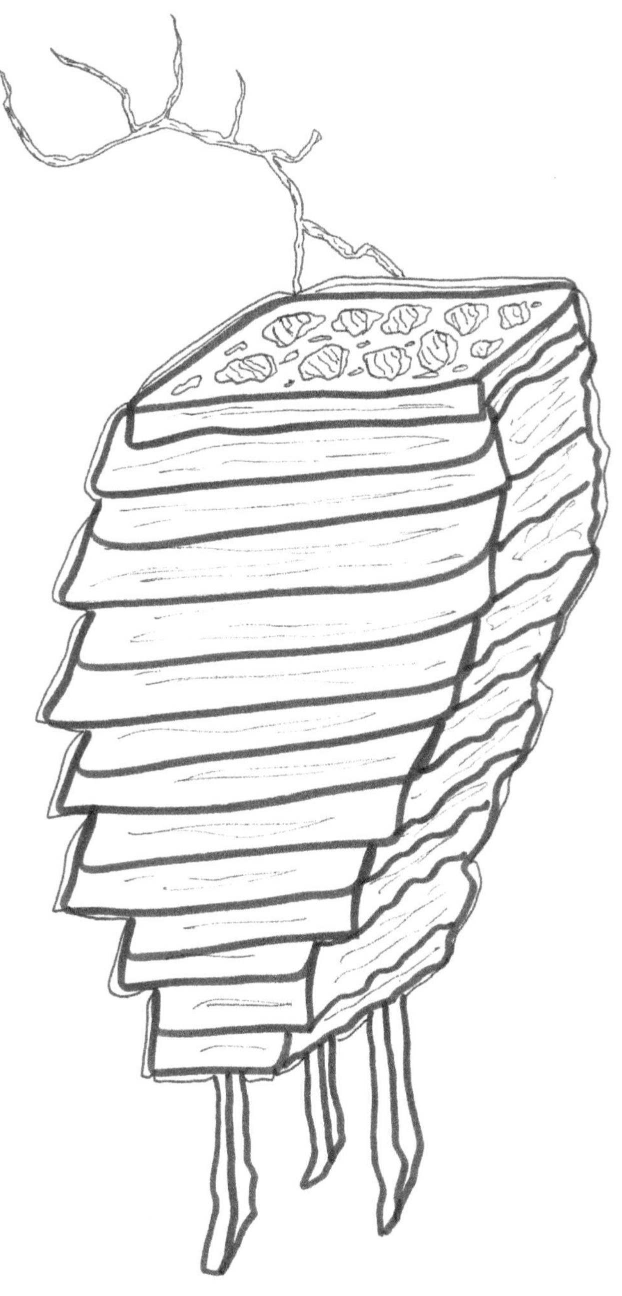

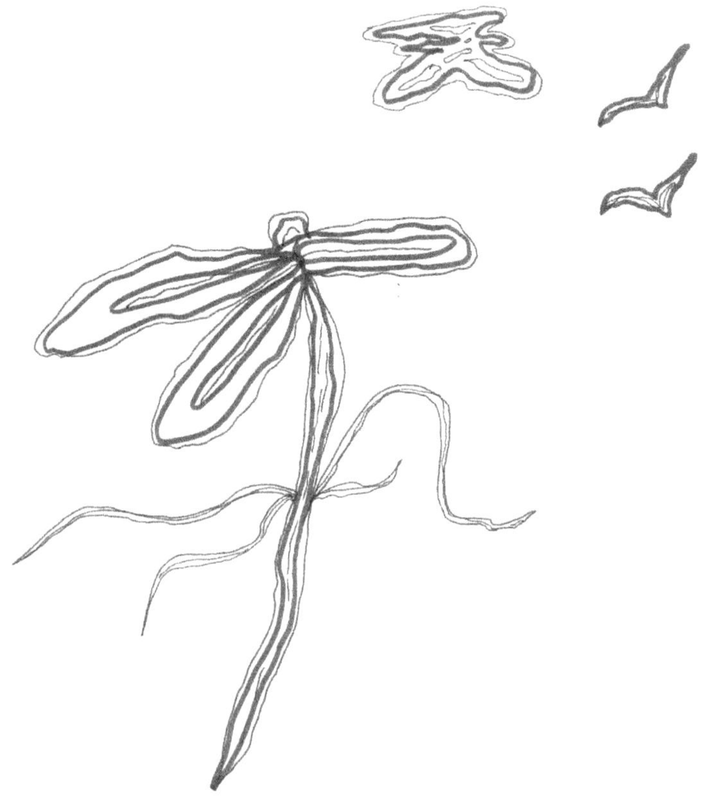

HOLD THE LIGHT • Rachel Delgado

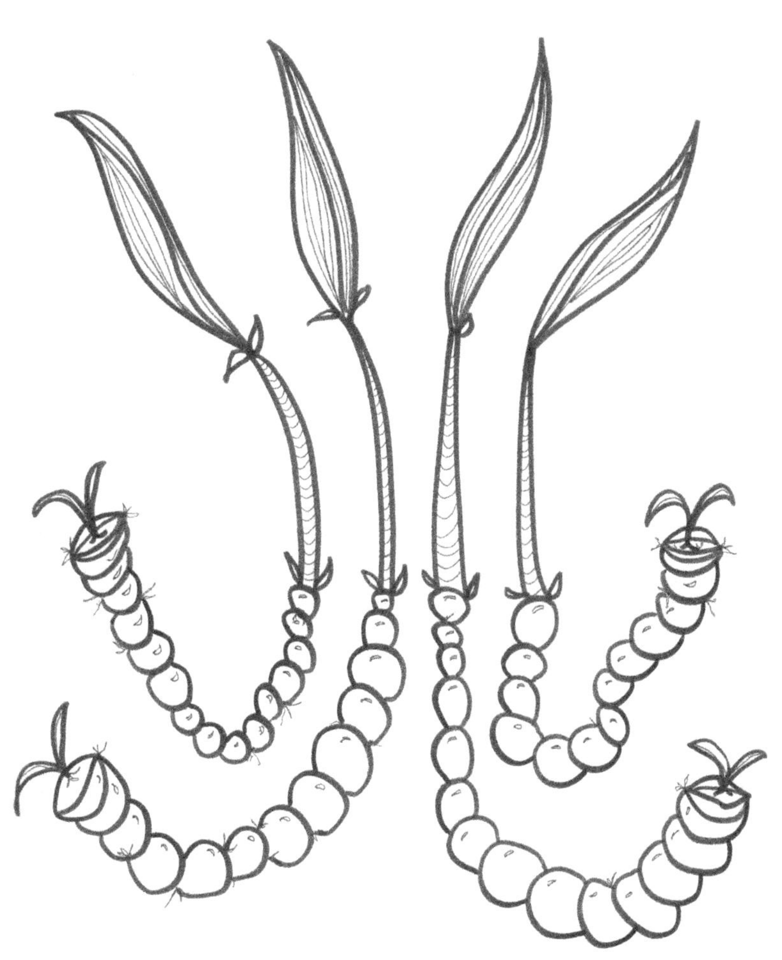

Alone, not lonely
Don't watch me cry
My tears are like a tender sigh
To free me from life's sharp goodbye
Each breath
A new found lullaby

Alone, not lonely
You'll often see
Creation cast a mystery
To one's delight and reverie
With silent sound
And memory

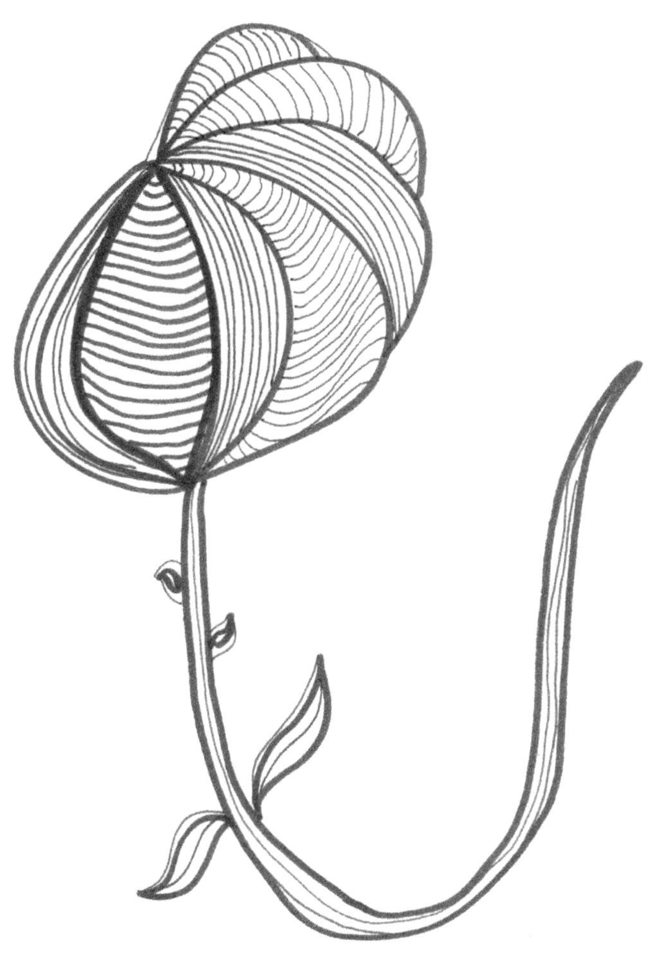

Soft and kind
As hearts align
To sow and reap
Let go and keep

How fast does time
Slow and speed
Outlast the time
To want or need

Through the age
Turning leaves
Brown or gray
Or yellow or green
Shining candles
Coincidence
I'm found again
In innocence
In truth and trust
My heart can see
And feel and hear
The mystery
Life reborn
Newness finally found

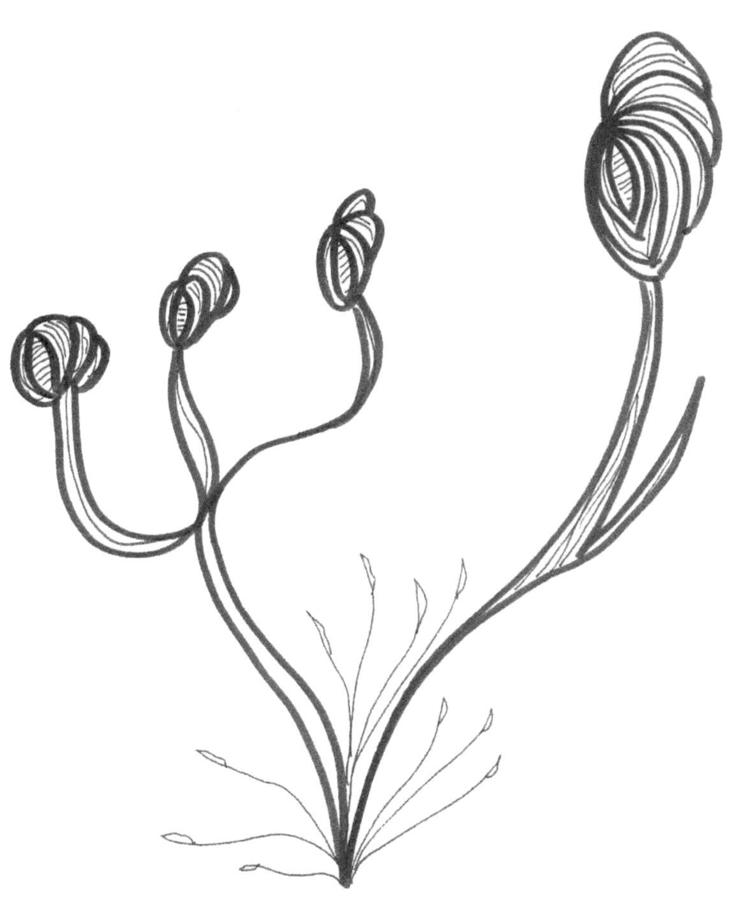

Look another vision
Comes to life's decisions
The way within
A song begins
Love's blessings to be given

Open paths to freedom
Appearing when we see them
Liberate
The wings of fate
The past finally forgiven

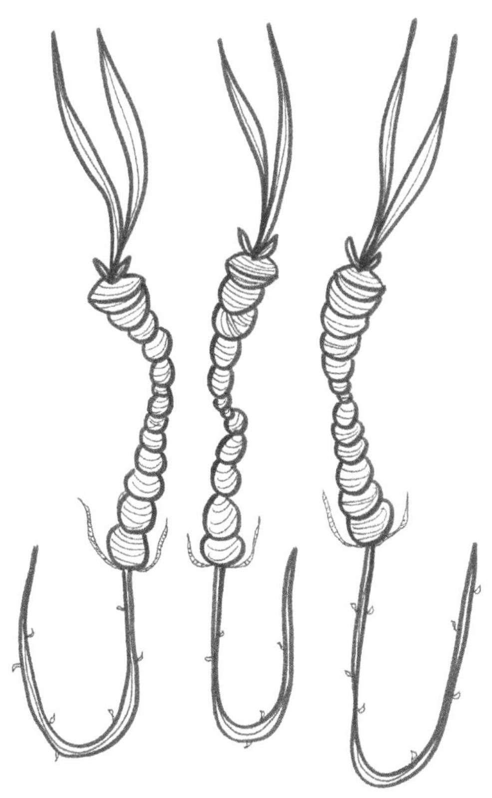

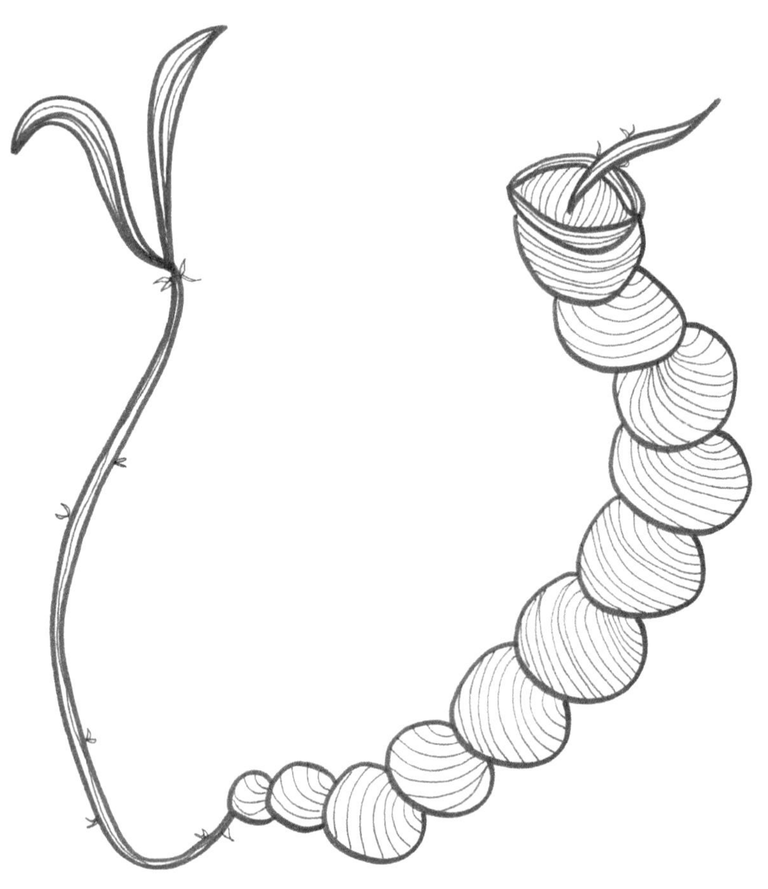

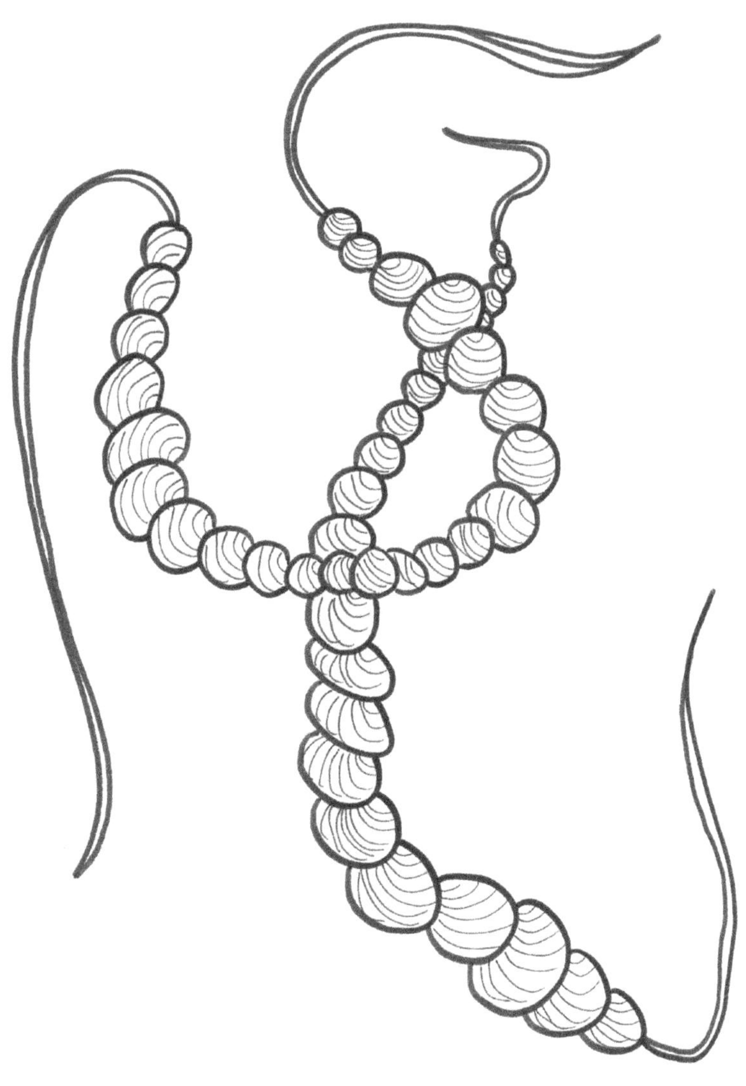

When I'm gone
Sing my song
And then yours
And then two more
That make your heart sing
When I'm gone

It will all subside
The rain falls down again
It will all come back
For another moment
And begin again
When I'm gone

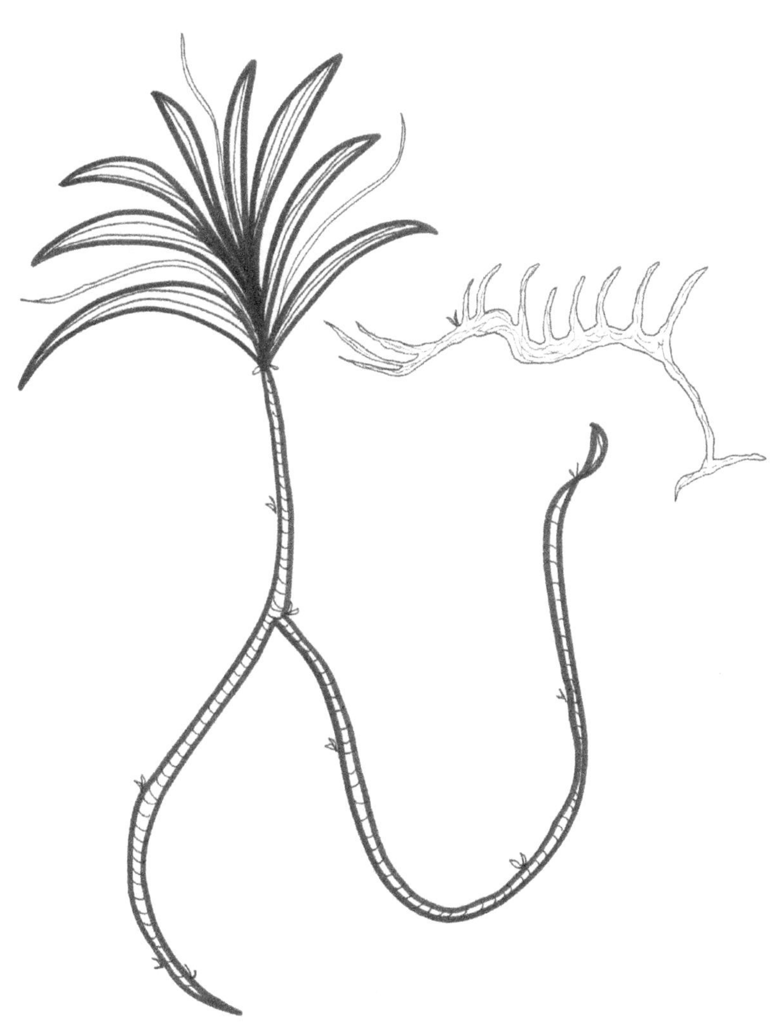

Can there be another me
Someone with the eyes to see
Innocent, divine, carefree
Everything she's meant to be

Will there be another way
For people by her side to say
How much they cared
Throughout the day
How they'd pray the pain away

Has there been another dream
Without the hurt
Without the schemes
Where happiness and love prevail
Greatness of a life unveiled

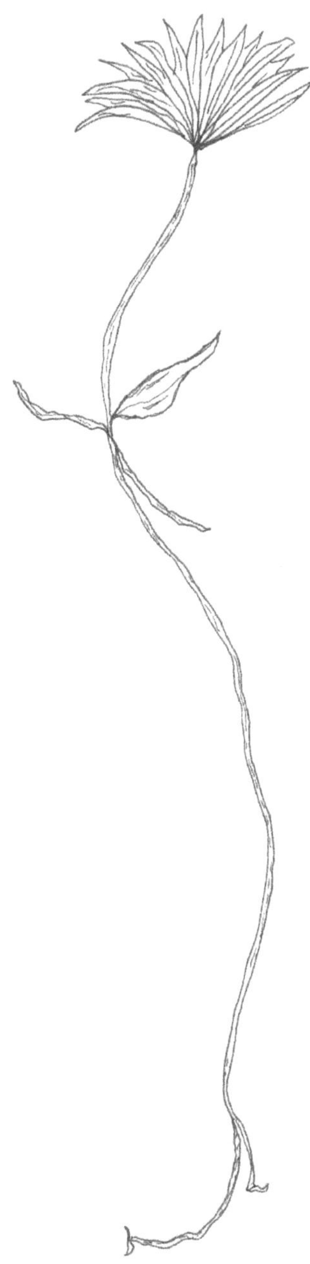

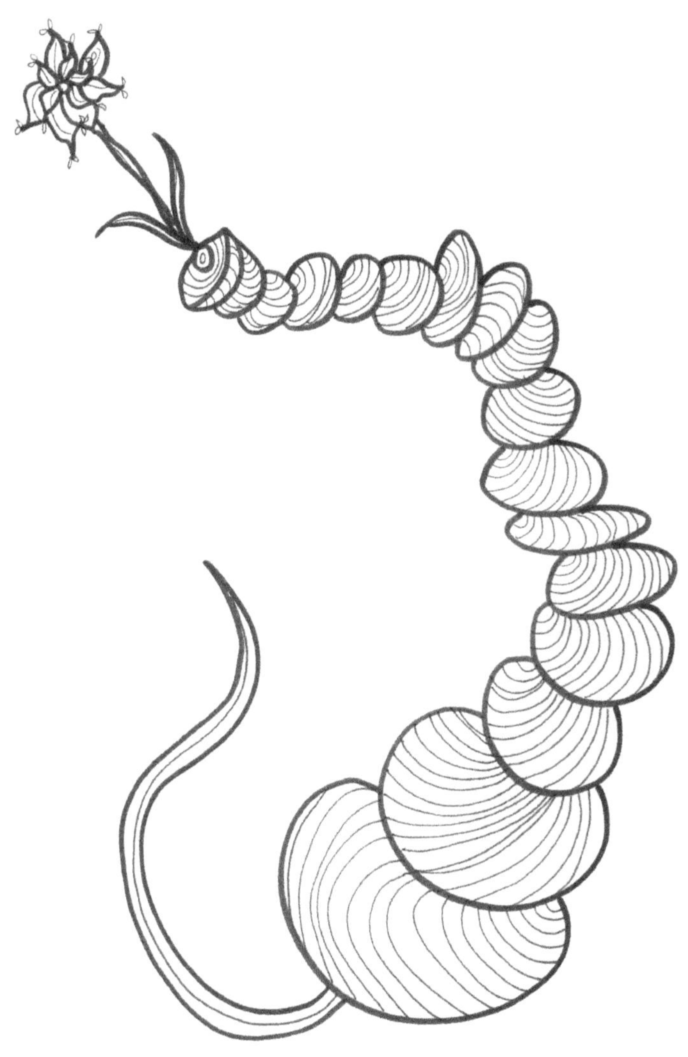

A boat to sail
Steadfast
A hand to hold
Comfort
Four walls
Four doors
Lock and key

Mountaintops
Trails to blaze
Silent sunsets
Rest
Two hearts
Four feet
Lock and key

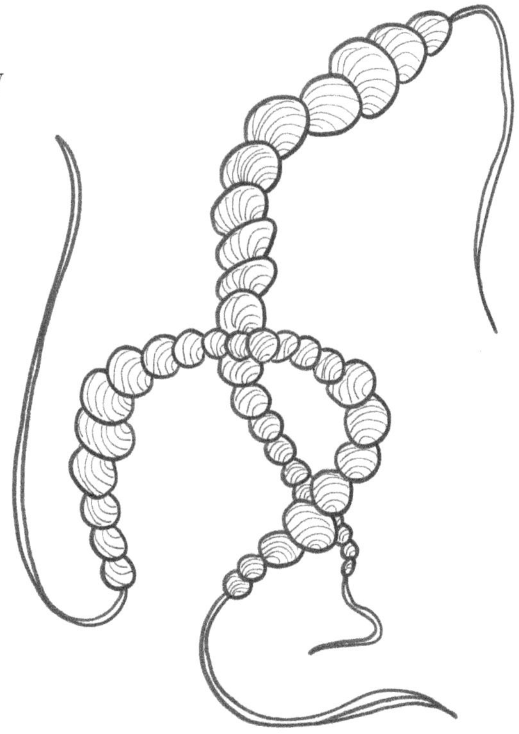

Steady rain
　Winter brisk
　　A bird with wings
　　　Lifted to the sky
　　　　Sitting majestically
　　　　Worn gray concrete
　　　　A steady being
　　　　　On grounded feet

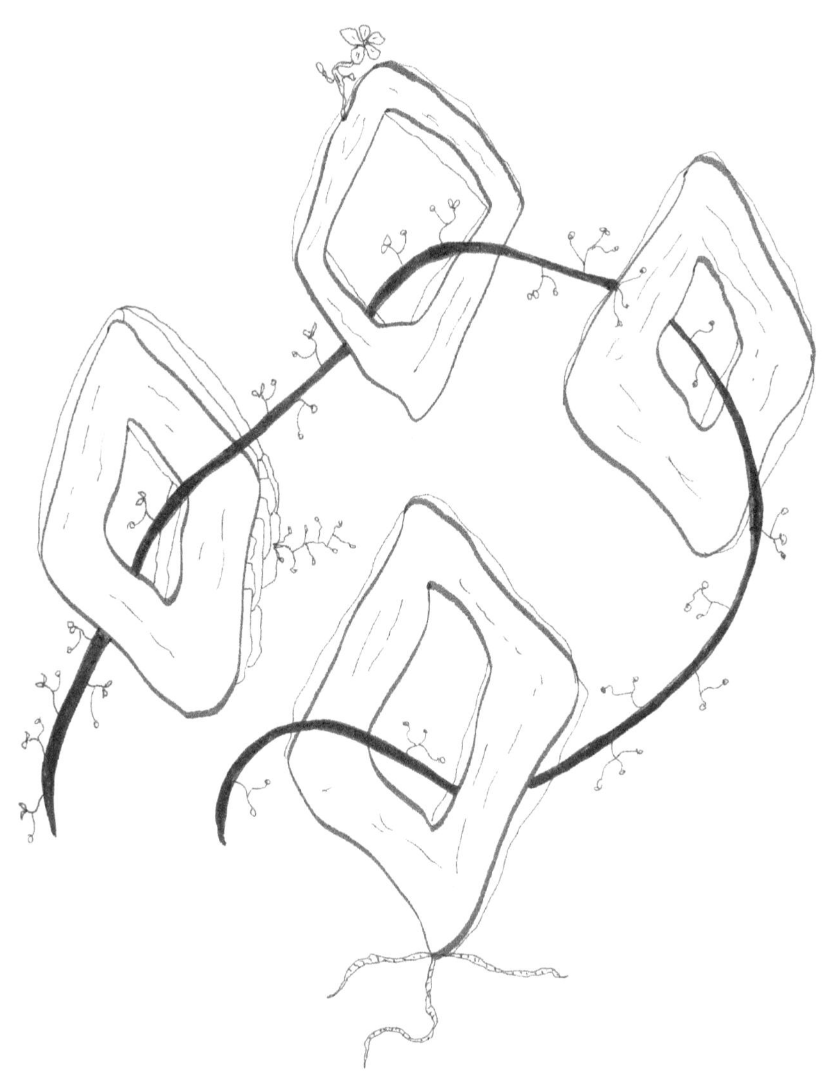

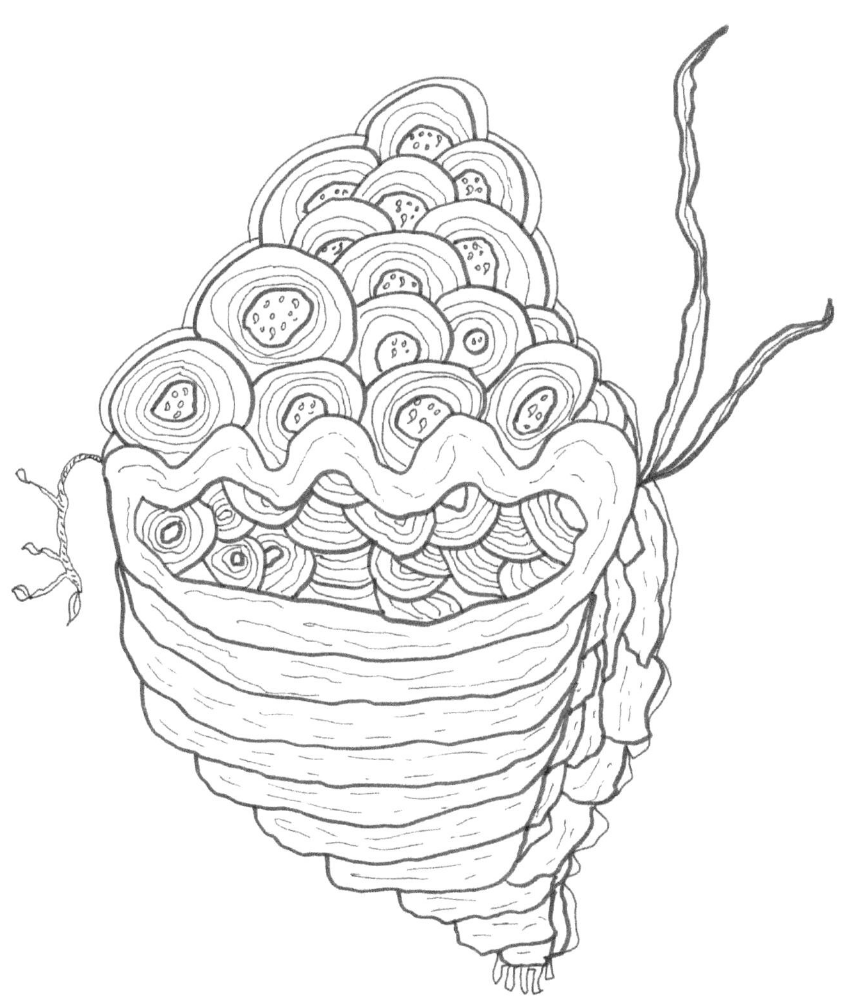

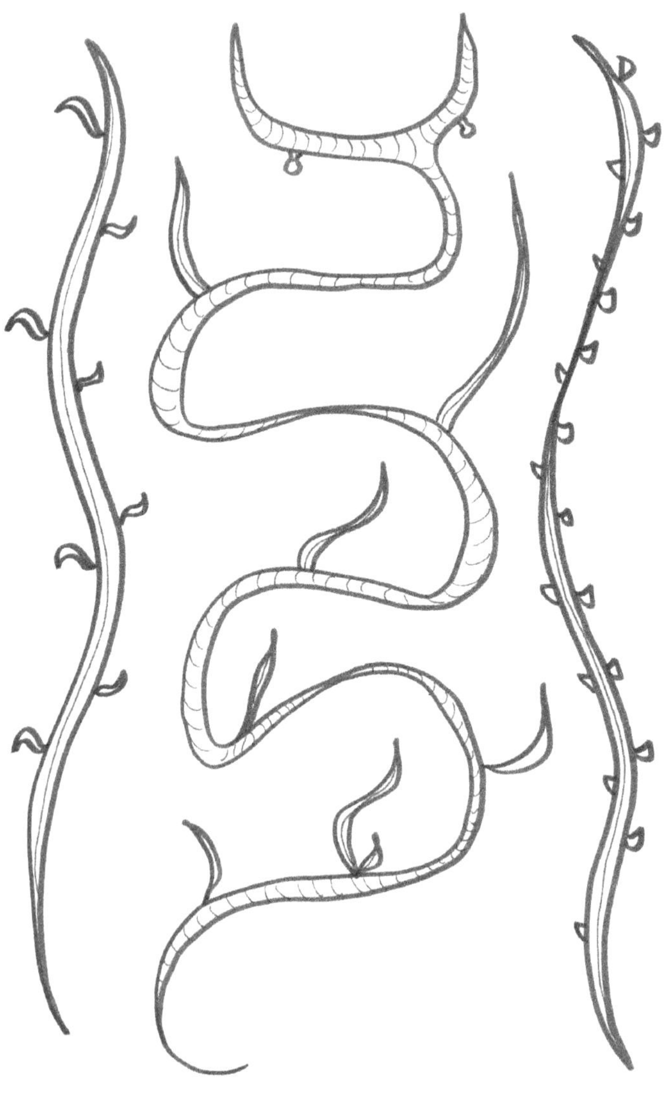

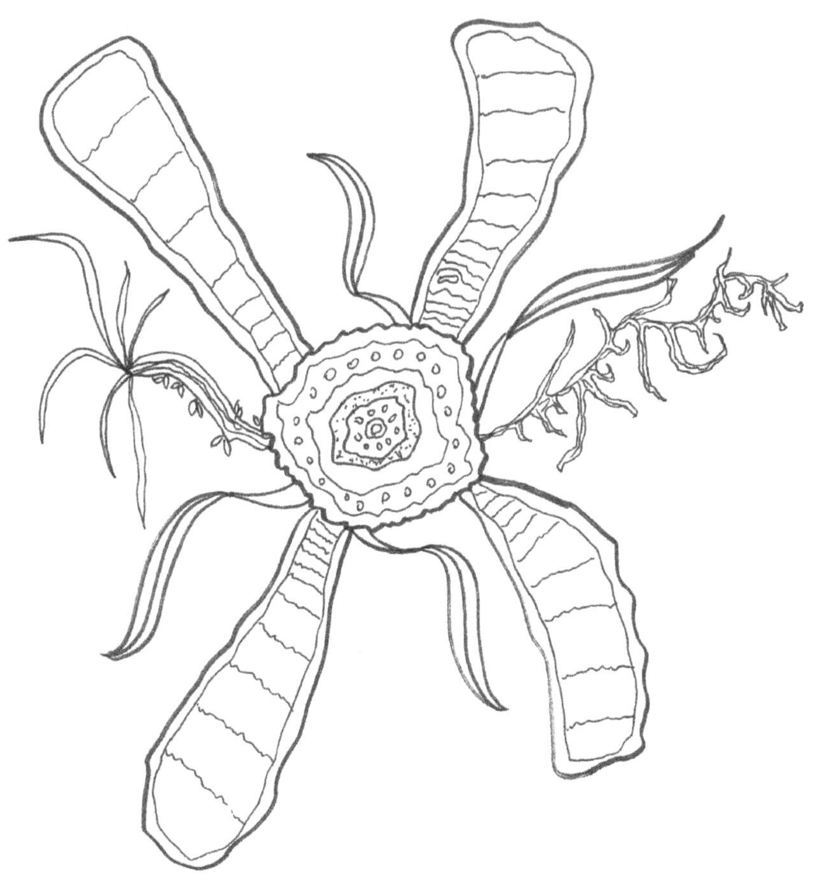

California, they said
Where it never rains
Would warm every cold and quivering soul
They said
Totally normal
Sensationally twisted
It's normal, they said
Steins to stains
Thoughts to brains
Waves to water
Mother to daughter
Pray to God, she said
The angel sat beside my bed
Dare to follow where you're led
Greens on trees of evergreen
In my California dream
Everything not as it seems
Strings on sticks
Gold and greed
Ocean foam
Planted seed

Protection
Tender care
Soothing
Divinity

Pacifying
Tending
Seeing
Delivering

Prayer
Truth
Strength
Dreams

Power
Trust
Softness
Dignity

Pull out the rusty knives
Where time stood still
And life wasn't found
One by one
The burn and sting
Won't erase
A memory
Or trace
Of wrongdoing
Or harm
But healing can begin

Extract the rusty nails
Hammered into days and years
Decades
A lifetime
Stained and torn
Dripping in doubt
Fervent agony

Slow unfolding
In newness of time
Knives and nails
Lay beside
A lifted body
Rust to dust
Disintegrate

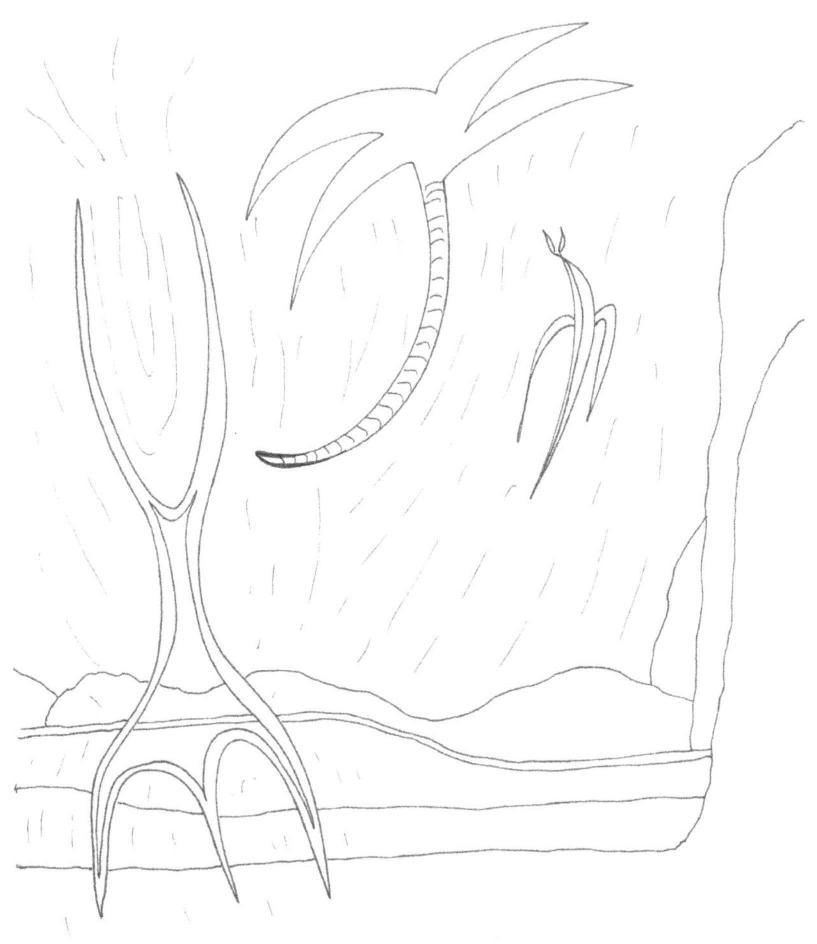

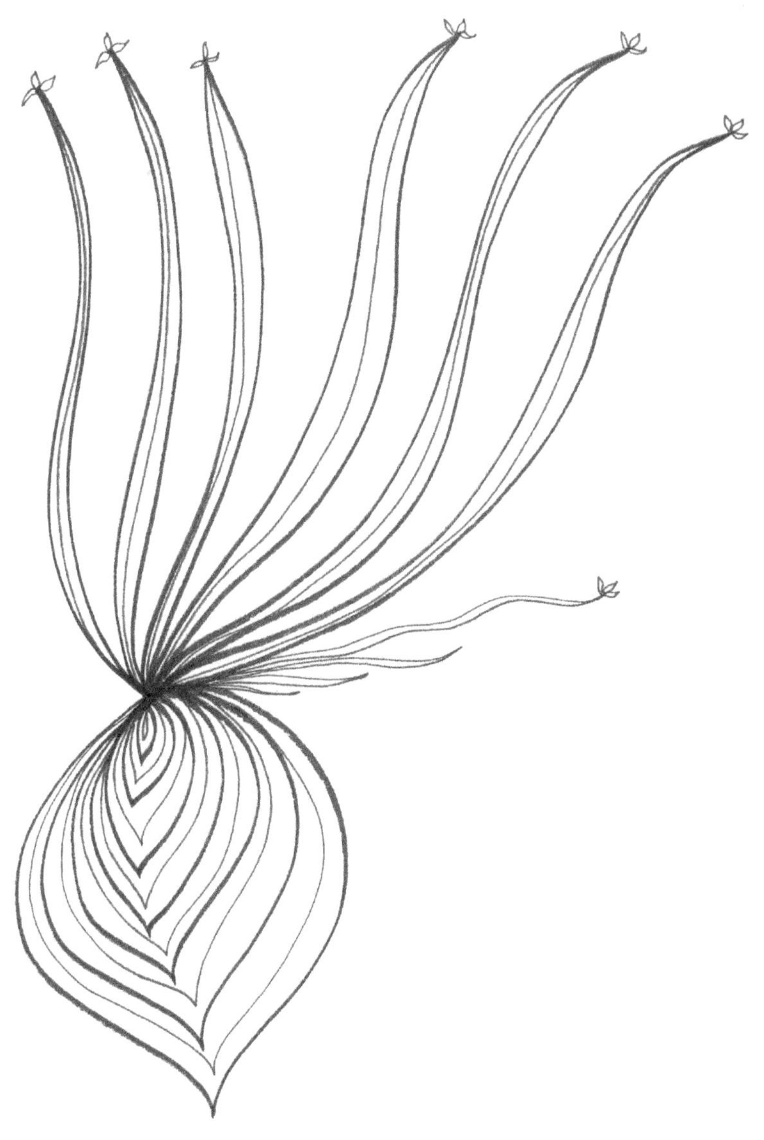

Deep underground
Beneath a cracked surface
A sprouted little one
Stretching for life
Longing for transformation
Sighs in separation
The sun reaches down
Bending to reflect
Mirrored images
In constant flux
All meeting at once
An instant chemistry
Igniting colors yet to be seen
In all directions
The connection floats on
Spinning in infinity
Making no sound

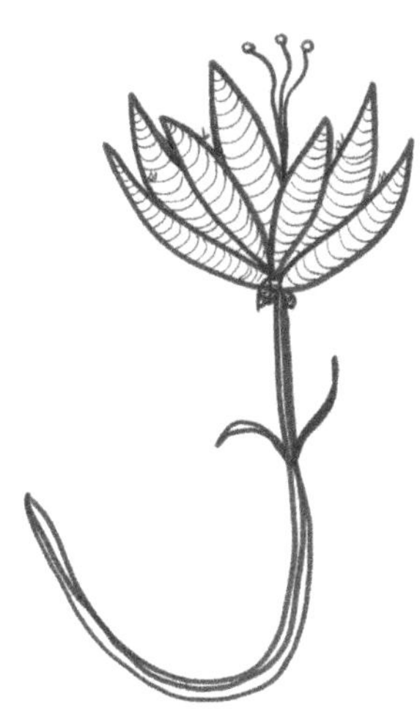

Sing along
Signs of spring
Whispering
Yellow green
Crystalline

Frankincense
Planted seed
Paths to lead
Sun and rain
Promised gain

Strengthened roots
Blaze the trail
The truth unveiled
Bamboo shoots
And arrowroot
A boat set sail
A holy grail

Open eyes
Your strength inside
Will never die
Okay to cry
When hope runs dry
The bird will sing
A lullaby

All will stand in reverie
The sky, the planets' harmony
See the you
That you can be

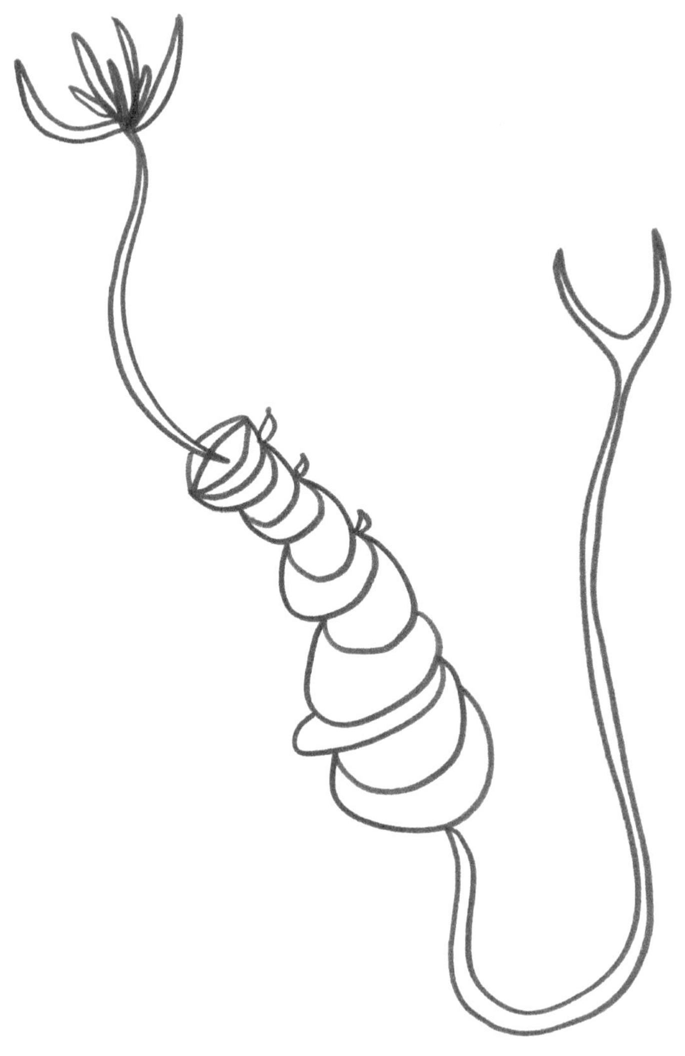

Own the life
Hurt and strife
Fade away
In disarray
Evaporated misery
Finding greater liberty
Herds and birds
Songs with words
Into one
Deliverer
Joy
Bliss
Chrysalis
Granted wish
Inner peace
The voice sets sail
Sea and wind
In harmony
All-knowing
Glowing
Opportunity
Flourishing
Rippling
Energy
Magnified
Sanctified
Majesty

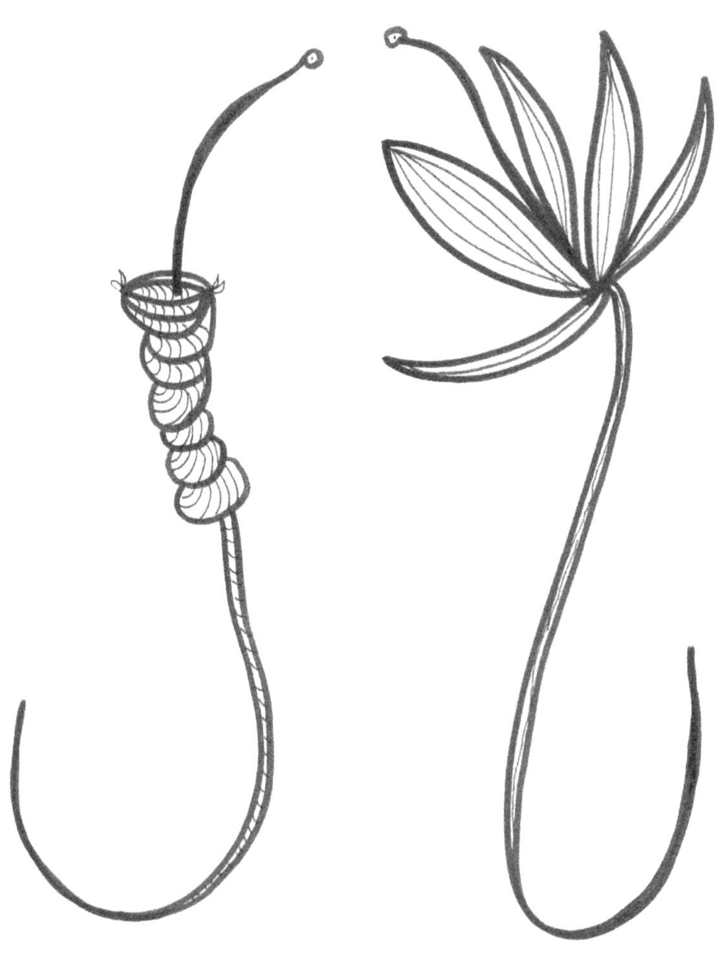

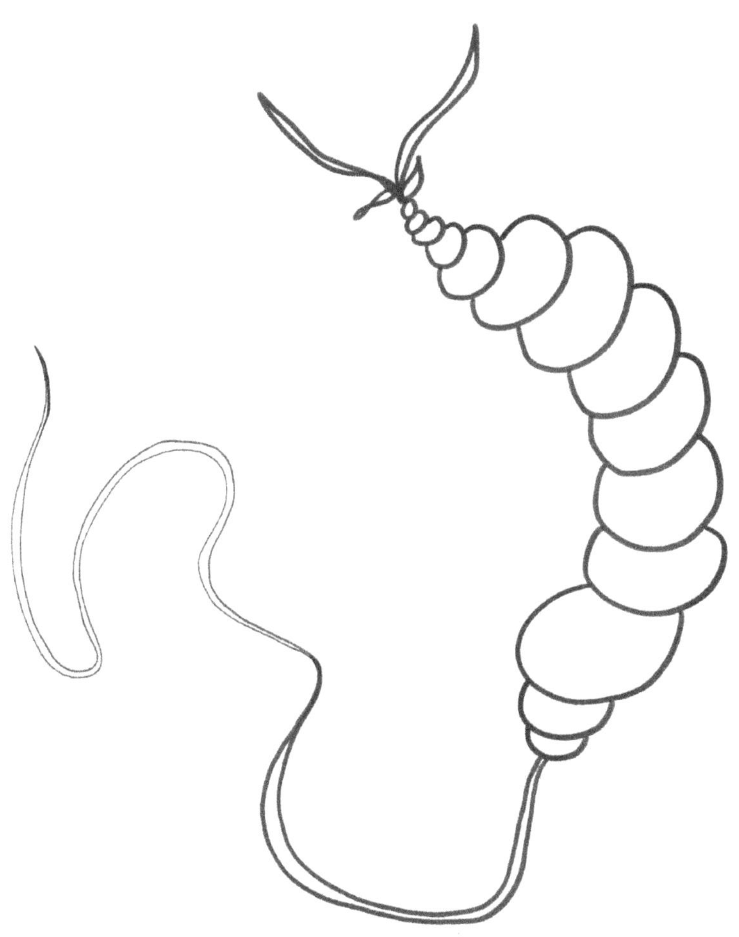

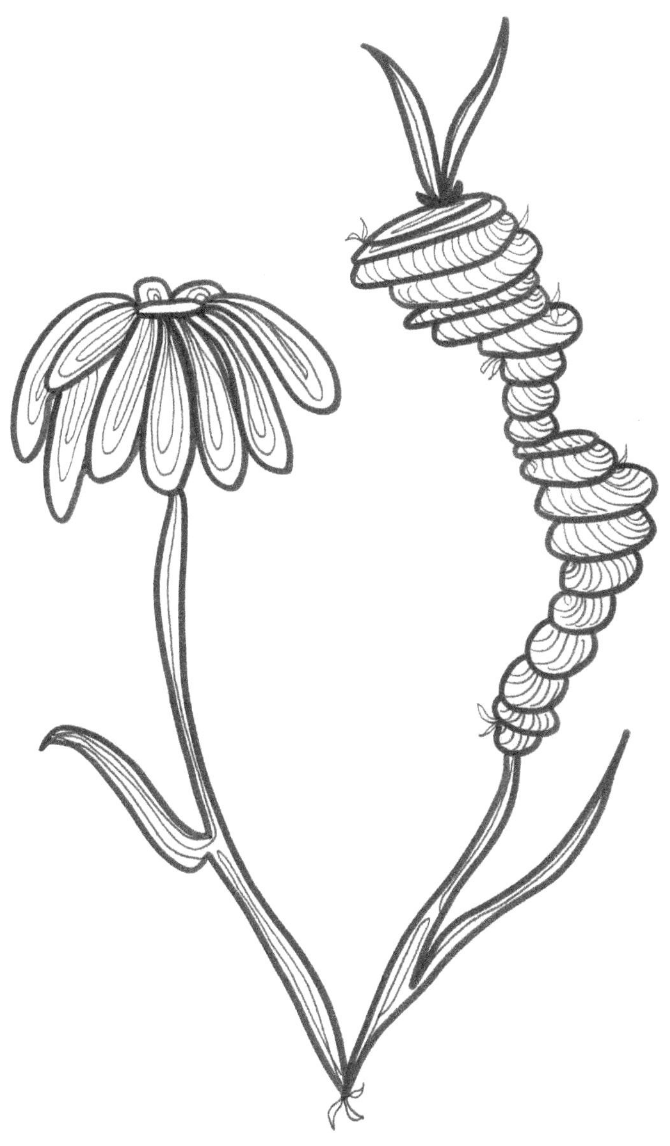

Pretty pictures
Celebrity fixtures
Age old programs
Knives is cold hands
Tense sensations
Hidden vibrations
Condemnation
Blood on gray skin
Colored glasses
Stolen passes
Going down
Kicking and screaming
Humankind
Reward reaping
Genuine
A look within
A quiet win
An inner grin
Wounds that heal
Dreams now real
Sign that's sealed
A world revealed

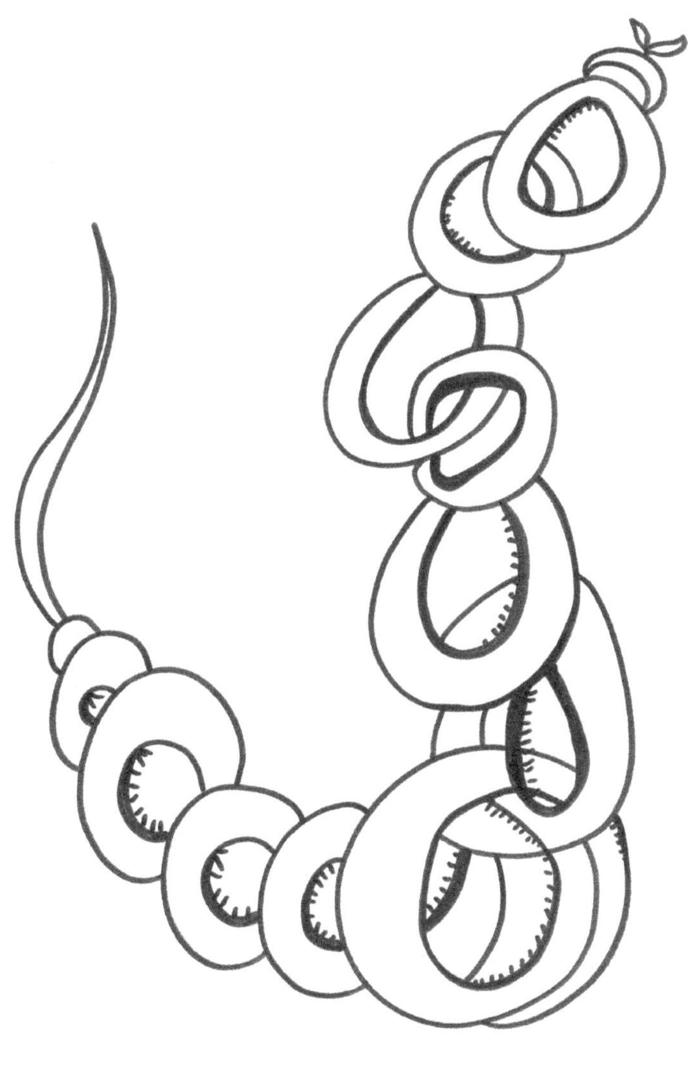

Beyond the comfort zone
Why let life pass you by
One step
Two steps
'Til it's alright
Believe
Receive it all
For light
Imaginings
Vanishing thoughts
Enough
To propel us
Forward

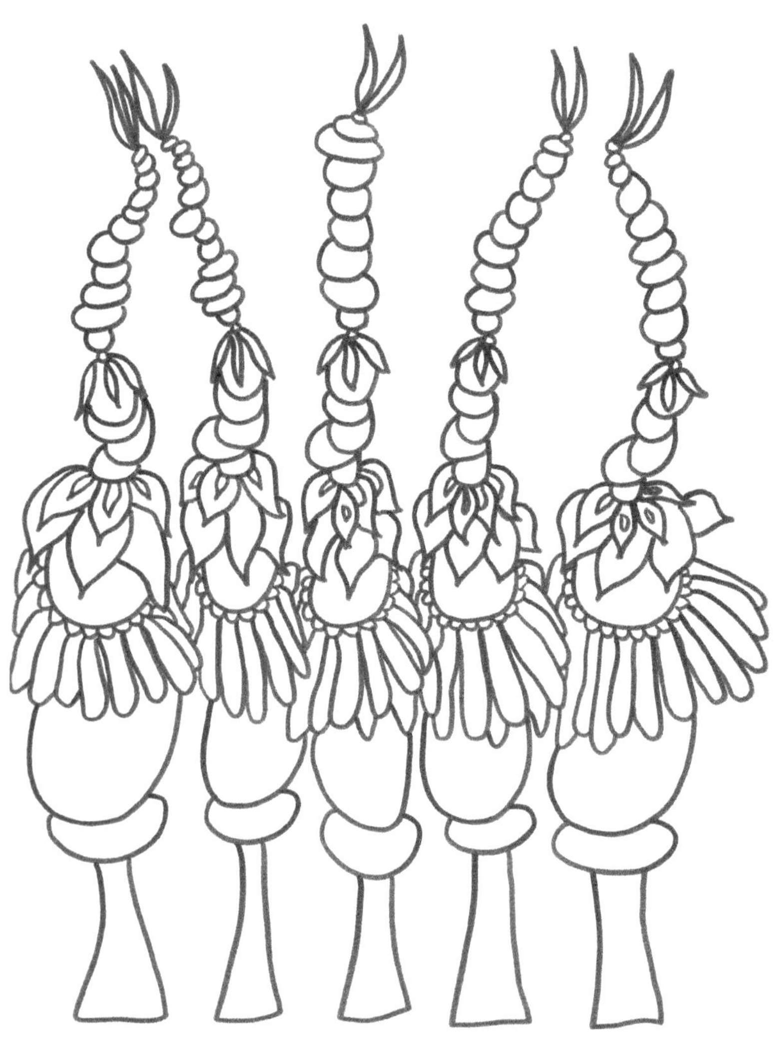

Affirming
Igniting
Liberating
Freedom

Singing
Soaring
Winning
Delight

Breathing
Stretching
Knowing
Being

Growing
Healing
Giving
Receiving
Strength

Inner
Subtle
Sitting
Peace

Traversing vast distances
Multitudes of instances
Annihilation
Love's creation
Princesses and princes

Gravity that pulls and lifts
Making valleys, lakes and rifts
Concentration
Timespace station
Means for giving gifts

Waves and force set life in motion
A sound that spans across the ocean
Strong connection
Same affection
Beyond any logic notion

Referencing a limited state
Possibly a test of fate
Information
Integration
Not much longer now to wait

Profound mechanics reverberate
All the things to celebrate
Innovating
Liberating
New ways to communicate

Music as a steady hand
Crashing waves upon the sand
Resonating
Commemorating
No one in command

Iron, carbon, oxygen
It can just begin again
Simmering
Shimmering
Life without an end

Your eyes are like diamonds
Your smile
The sun rising
Your touch
A summer day

You're like a piano
Wherever the wind blows
Your flight is the light in the dark

You're a star
Shimmering
Where you are
I'll follow

Your eyes are like diamonds
Your smile
The sun rising
Your touch
A summer day

Shine where you are

What joy to see your beauty
What joy to see your eyes
What joy to love you simply
What joy you give my life

How flawless is your beauty
What joy in soft delight
My heart will sing how lovely
What joy you give my life

You are love
You're worthy
In this light
Where you are free
In your eyes
I am worthy
In this light
Where we are free

Who moves the mountains
Slices, carves and tatters
What lifts leaves and petals
Against nature's force for falling

Boats float
Planes fly
Higher still
Truth denied

Oasis desert
Thirst for good
What flag raises
Spirit and justice

Black turns to light
People shout
Bones, feelings
Rising tide
Deception, reverie
Powered up
Strengthening within
Igniting

Sing the finest song you know
Dance until you start to glow
Happiness within to grow
Anywhere you want to go

I can feel the energy
Something calling to be free
Shining, bright and shimmery
Showing me what I can be

In the midst of affection and love
If all my thoughts hold true
The mess of reality
And ever-changing tide
Fade away with you beside
My soul's content
And life's reward
In you
And love
And loving more

Laying
Wait
To sleep
At night
The dark
Holds fast
Commanding
Light

Tender
Care
Soft
Desire
Ripping
Through
Burnt
Desire

Touch
Infused
Divine
Adventure
Inward
Youth
Seed
Hope
Power

Fell soft upon the tide
That's the nature sometimes
Of a love that cannot divide
And though it's past
And plenty gained
What's lost and broken
Cannot remain
For heart embattled
With disdain
And draught with laughter
Pleasure veins
Emotions deep
In awesome valor
What's mighty steadfast
New found hour

Hold without attachment
Sold without a cash in
Stand on feet surrounded
Energized and grounded

Hold by letting go
White like winter snow
Empty for abundance filled
Strength of a foundation built

Hold for you and no one else
Hold on to the love of self
Shine the light within the heart
Every moment ways to start

Light up what you know is true
Everything is here for you
Give yourself the grace to live
Letting go of what it is
That bounds us to unhappiness
That causes hurtfulness and stress
Hold the light within to shine
Fullness of a love divine

Green leaves fluttering
From misty drifts on mountains
Elevated winds

Picture me
In reverie
On the sea
The seaweed green
Fresh and clean
Steadily
The salty breeze
Enforces ease
Realized dream

Spring

Green pastures
Running horses
Resolutions and resources
Boundless beauty
Strength of sources
Unimaginable forces

Follow self to fresh spring water
As a mother and a daughter
Overflowing life's rewarder
For a living, breathing author

Go within to find the spring
Sing the song you love to sing
For it's grace and
light and hope
you bring
Like a gentle wind
that's whispering

Strong and steady
Hold your ground
Armed and ready
Hear the sound
Light the fire
Set it free
You be you
For now
Just be

Homeostasis
Lifted faces
Spaces of graces
Higher places
Ground that shakes us
Molds and makes us
Reach for higher
Steady fire
Walk in light
Clearing sight
An open door
Forevermore

Leaves fall
Gentle like the wind
Rain's aroma
Permeating the air
Soil and grass
Soaking seeds
Broken branches
The bite of cold
Breathing in
Opening
In love with life
In the falling leaves

Skies purple, orange
Sighing clouds
Prickly branches
Swaying in the wind
Bending without breaking
The sea calls a lonely soul
Broken from scattered shards
The magnetism of fate's desire
Trembling in excitement
Wave to water
Mother to daughter
Life's bliss whispers
I'll answer

ACKNOWLEDGMENTS

My heartfelt gratitude to my loving husband EJ for being an inspiration and supporting me in speaking my truth. Thanks to all my friends and family for lifting me up through the years. Thanks to my father and sister for the strength, love and support through the curving paths of life. Thanks to my grandmother for everything she did for our family, and to my mother for bringing me here and teaching me so much in such a short time. Thanks to all my mentors and guides along the way. The journey continues with appreciation for all who have shown immense love and care in these precious times.

ABOUT THE AUTHOR

Rachel Delgado is a musician, composer, and artist from Las Vegas, NV. She is founder of Musicians Peer Support, a community of creatives supporting the independent arts, and is co-owner of Wave Squad Music House, a music production company with composer and guitarist EJ Delgado, whose music can be heard worldwide. Rachel continues to perform and compose music, write poetry and develop her artistry, while supporting others in living their dreams.